BRICK-AND-MORTAR ISN'T DEAD

BRICK
-AND-
MORTAR
ISN'T DEAD

HOW TO RUN
A SUCCESSFUL
CUSTOMER-CENTRIC
BUSINESS
FROM LAUNCH
TO EXPANSION

JASON WILSON

LIONCREST
PUBLISHING

BRICK-AND-MORTAR ISN'T DEAD
How to Run a Successful Customer-Centric
Business from Launch to Expansion

ISBN   978-1-61961-884-8 *Paperback*
   978-1-61961-883-1 *Ebook*

CONTENTS

———

INTRODUCTION

———

I'm the proud owner of Riverside Pawn, a chain of seven stores that loans out more than $10 million a year, thanks to a customer-centric business model.

Climbing the ranks in this industry hasn't been easy. In the early days, the odds definitely seemed stacked against me, and I often wish I'd had a resource like this book to show me the way. It would have prevented me from making some of the mistakes I've made over the years.

You see, I never finished high school and didn't go to college. I was a terrible student, all Ds and Fs. I was socially awkward and lazy. I didn't care about anything. My parents worked in bad jobs for below-average income, and for a while, we lived in a trailer park. Because of our poverty, we never had much food and didn't have an air conditioner or heater. That might not sound like the origin story of a successful business owner, but I consider the way I grew up as a badge of honor.

Why? Because it has provided me with the motivation I need to keep going in the face of every hardship and challenge. I don't worry about failing in business. I'm not afraid to embarrass myself or lose money. My only fear is that my kids might experience the kinds of things I went through, and that fear drives me to make sure they have a better life. Being scared of poverty has kept me off my butt, working hard to earn everything I have, and building my business.

PLAYING TO YOUR STRENGTHS AND PASSIONS

Not everything in my childhood was poverty and pain. I learned some important skills that have served me well over the years. If you want to be an entrepreneur, then you need to choose something that caters to your strengths, something you're passionate about. The core of my business is obtaining used goods and selling them for a profit. It's something I learned to do at a young age.

My dad and I bonded over comic books and baseball cards, and we attended conventions to buy and sell vintage comics and cards. Hustling at the conventions became our weekend business, and I quickly developed a real passion for it. Despite our low income, my dad had a strong work ethic. He worked six or seven days a week at his job, and then he worked the conventions. That's how I learned that if you want to be successful, you must earn it.

Going to conventions on the weekends became my part-time job. It gave me a chance to watch my dad, spend time with him, and make money doing it. I also learned to develop relationships with people, interacting one-on-one as we bought and sold. When I got older, around twelve or thirteen, my best friend and I went to conventions on our own. My parents would drop us off, and we would set up a table to sell our own merchandise. I enjoyed it, and, in a way, it's what I'm still doing today, just on a bigger scale.

School just wasn't my motivation, and eventually I dropped out. Aside from selling at conventions, I worked a series of dead-end jobs with no real long-term prospects. My life was going nowhere because I hadn't yet learned how to play to my strengths.

Things began to change around the time I turned twenty. I was still living with my parents when I came across a classified ad for part-time help at a local pawn shop. I applied, got the job, and took to the work right away. The business was a small operation. I stayed for seven years and began to develop my own ideas about how to run the store and tweak the business. The pawn business became my passion in the same way that selling at conventions did years earlier.

As you might know, the pawn business has a lot of negative stereotypes and stigmas. Think about how pawn shops are portrayed in movies and television: back alley operations in poorly lit neighborhoods, bars on the windows and doors, run by shady people hunkered behind dingy counters, places where criminals lurk in corners and where stolen goods are the daily fare.

IT'S ALL ABOUT RELATIONSHIPS

That's Hollywood's view of the pawn business, but I didn't see it that way. I saw a huge opportunity to change the perception. While the owner seemed driven solely by a desire to make as much money as possible off each customer, I saw a business providing a meaningful service. I dreamed of a better approach. What if our primary purpose was to help people? What if we committed to providing real value for customers, creating long-term relationships, instead of just trying to make money?

What if we created relationships with customers that lasted for years, earning their trust through excellent and compassionate service? Making money would become the byproduct of helping our customers, a happy result of a carefully crafted relationship.

I began to share this vision of the business with the pawn shop owner and the other workers. At first, they smiled and shrugged it off. I'm sure I seemed naïve and idealistic, a silly young man thinking too big. Their attitude was, "When a customer brings in an item, buy it as low as you can and sell it as high as you can." When I pressed the issue, when I refused to drop the subject, they started getting irritated. That led to heated discussions, which turned to arguments, and eventually, the owner and I had a huge falling out.

We'd gotten close by that point, hanging out as friends, even taking vacations together, but he finally said, "Look, I don't think we can work together. You're clearly not happy here. Neither of us is enjoying this, so let's just separate and do our own thing."

I learned the hard way that when you're working for someone, your hands are tied. You can't make major decisions about a business when it's not yours.

MY ONE PATH

Despite my frustrations with the way the business had been run, I'd fallen in love with the pawn industry. I didn't have any other training. Yet that small shop was the only one in town. I remember sitting in my house the night I lost the job, staring at a stack of monthly bills, desperately trying to figure out what to do with my life. The pawn business was something I enjoyed and was good at, and I instinctively knew it was my one path forward.

One way or another I had to open my own shop. It was my only chance to realize my growing vision for how pawn shops should be run. I wanted to open a store that would become the standard by which all others were judged—if not nationally, then at least locally. I had no idea how to do that, but I made the decision to try that night.

SHAPE YOUR OWN REALITY

All I had in the beginning was a goal, but I set the goal and bought into it fully. Maybe you've heard the old saying, "Whether you think you can do it or not, you're probably right." It's true; you can determine your own success. My commitment to the goal shaped my reality in the years that followed, through all of the hardships I experienced. I'm convinced we can only accomplish what we envision, and what we believe we can accomplish. Fear of failure holds us back. If you're afraid to do something, you're less likely to take the first step.

Back then, there was no social media, only dial-up internet, so I had no easy way to research how to open a business. In those days, if you wanted to research a subject, you had to go down to the local library or a bookstore and try to find a real book that could help you. I had absolutely no idea where to start. Remember, I had less than a high school diploma. I definitely had no formal training on starting a business. All I could do was play it by ear and try to learn on the go.

Of course, all the research in the world wouldn't have been enough because I was trying to do something new and different. I wanted to run my business with a very specific vision: a pawn shop that focused on cultivating relationships with customers instead of focusing solely on making money. I had to figure that out myself and make it work.

The night I decided to do this, I had exactly $1,872 in my bank account. That's not nearly enough to start a business, so I needed a loan. The only experience I had working with a bank was getting a home mortgage, so I called the loan officer who had helped me with that. I explained that I'd left my job and wanted to open my own store. He didn't sound excited, but he asked me to draw up a business plan and bring it to him. I had no idea how to draw up a business plan. I'd never seen one before., but I sat down at my computer, opened up a Word document, and started typing. I wrote down how much money I thought I needed, why I needed it, how I intended to make the money back, and how long I thought it would take. I didn't know if that's what he wanted to see, but it was all the information I had.

What I wound up with didn't look very professional, but I took it with me to my meeting at the bank two days later. The loan officer reviewed the document. He'd already checked my bank balance and credit report. As I sat there, watching him read my crude business plan, I felt super nervous. Finally, he set the paper down and looked at me.

"You have very little credit history," he said, "and now you have no job. You have less than $2,000 in the bank, and your business plan is asking for a $100,000 loan. There's just no way I can help you."

It stung, but I had hyped myself up for this meeting. I was determined to convince this guy to give me the money I needed to open my business, one way or the other. I decided to try bluffing him.

"Okay, you don't have to loan me the money," I replied, "but I am going to get it somewhere. I'll keep asking. I'll ask at every bank in town. Eventually, someone will loan me the money, and when they do, I'm going to open my store. And I'm not just going to open one store. I'll expand to multiple stores, and whoever helps me do that, I'll be loyal to that person and that bank for the next thirty years. They'll help me become successful, and they'll make a lot of money off me in the process. If that doesn't interest you, so be it."

I don't think he bought it, but I finally wore him down.

He looked at me, sighed, and said, "Okay, look, you have $20,000 worth of equity in your house, so here's my offer: sell your cars to get rid of the car payments, and I can get you a $30,000 home equity loan. It's not as much as you wanted, but it's the best I can do."

I took him up on the offer and ran with it. That loan is what started my first business, and here I am, thirteen years later, and I've closed over $4 million in real estate deals. Through all of them, I've worked with that same loan officer at the same bank. I promised I would be a loyal customer, and I have been. What's the lesson? Don't take "no" for an answer when you're starting your business. Believe that there's a way to get it done, and then go out and find that way.

THREE STAGES OF BUSINESS

Based on my experience, I believe there are three basic stages to any business.

First, you go through a toddler phase, where the business consumes all of your time. It needs constant attention and care just to survive. You have to be there all the time, holding its hand, helping it grow, nurturing it every step of the way. If you turn your attention away even for a short time, something bad might happen. That requires a lot of patience, but it pays off in the long run.

The second phase comes when the business grows to the point where you can't handle it on your own. That's when you hire people. It's a huge step in any small business, but it brings about a transformation into the teenager phase. As a teen, your business still needs you, still requires guidance, but it's more mature and doesn't demand constant attention every second of the day.

Finally, if you stick with it long enough, you get to the adult phase, and you can now leave the business to other people. They run the business under the plan you've put in place, and you can move on and start the process all over again in a new location.

You might have a long way to go to get your business to the adult stage, but if you'll make the commitment to work hard, you'll get there. I'll show you the way, step by step. Are you ready?

PART ONE

THE TODDLER STAGE

CHAPTER ONE

GO ALL IN

———

A popular phrase in business circles goes something like this: "Entrepreneurship is living a few years of your life how others won't, so that you can live the rest of your life how others can't." It's true. Early on in your business, especially in the first "toddler" stage, you'll have to sacrifice many things in order to realize your long-term potential. There's no way around it; you can't half-ass anything and expect full results.

Some people, especially young people, see successful entrepreneurs on the internet or social media, people with financial freedom who enjoy great lifestyles, and they don't realize exactly what it takes to get there. They don't realize the massive sacrifices those successful people made, the huge risks they took, or the endless hours of hard work they put in. They want overnight success. They want the money right away.

PAYING YOUR DUES

I was no different. In the beginning, I didn't realize how many things I would have to give up in my personal life to make my business succeed, not until I got in and did it. What are the sacrifices you have to make? First, and maybe most significantly, you have to give up the sense of stability and security that comes from a normal job. The moment you decide to quit your regular job to open your own business, you give up a normal paycheck. That direct deposit every other Friday is no longer guaranteed. Money's not going to magically show up in your account now. You're also giving up paid sick leave and paid vacation. That's a huge sacrifice, and it can be really scary at first.

Think about it. You'll never get another paycheck in your life, unless you create it yourself through your business. Many people can't accept that—it's not society's norm. Society says you get a job, work nine to five, and get paid for it. Are you ready to give that up to take the leap in starting your own business? It can pay off in bigger ways down the road, but you'll have to deal with the instability for a while.

You also give up a lot of material things early on. In the beginning, every penny I could spare went right back into my business to help it grow. As I mentioned before, when I first applied for a loan, I had two car payments. In order to qualify for the loan, my wife and I had to sell those cars and buy something a lot cheaper. We wound up with an old $5,000 Toyota Celica. We drove it every day, sharing that one car. It was a huge downgrade, but it was something we had to do to give my business a chance to succeed. Not only that, but we sacrificed things like going out to dinner, going out to bars, and buying nice things.

All of the money we would have spent on those things went right back into the business. We didn't go to movies, we didn't have a social life, and we rarely ever went out—that's what it took. I didn't take a vacation for three years, rarely went to parties, and didn't go anywhere on the weekends. All of that was a waste of money, and I was so busy, I couldn't have kept up that lifestyle anyway. I needed to pour all of my energy into my business.

When you open a business, you're never off work. In those first few years, I was physically in the store from 9 a.m. to 6 p.m., six days a week, but even when I wasn't there, I spent time planning and preparing, thinking about ways to make things more efficient, to provide better value for my customers. I laid in bed every single night, thinking and planning. I was so obsessed with my business that I didn't want to do anything else. On those rare occasions when I found myself at a party or some fun event, I couldn't enjoy myself. I was too busy thinking about work the whole time.

I had no salary for three or four years. All I did was take a draw to pay personal bills. I had no extra money. This is a side effect of starting a business that many people don't think about. They see the glamour, all the excitement that goes along with owning your own business, but they don't consider the hardships. Giving up all of these things is hard, and a lot of people can't deal with it when it happens. Remember, it's about making short-term sacrifices that will pay off huge in the long run.

I've met so many entrepreneurs and business owners over the years, and they all say the same thing: "You have to sacrifice to be successful." You have to give up many things to focus on your business, but when you do that, you groom yourself for better things later on. Someday you'll achieve real success, and when you do, then you get to have all those fun things back. Then, you get to take nice vacations and drive nice cars. It's a "pay now, play later" philosophy. It's very difficult, but it's worth it. I mean, do you really want to give up long-term success for a little bit of short-term pleasure?

CHASE THE PASSION, NOT THE MONEY

Should you start your own business? Is it right for you? Do you possess the dedication to make it happen? Those are questions you must answer before you dive in and make the sacrifices. It's true of any business in any industry. We live in an age of e-commerce, where apps and websites like Amazon make it easier than ever to do business online. You order it today, and tomorrow it's on your doorstep.

I don't think e-commerce will ever completely take the place of brick-and-mortar stores, because there will always be value in building one-on-one relationships in business. People still crave face-to-face interaction. I can order a book off Amazon, but if I want to interact with real people, to walk around and chat, I have to go to my local bookstore. The one-on-one relationships you can develop at a local store will always be important to some people. What that means is, if you're going to start a brick-and-mortar store, you have to play to that strength.

From the days of the old general store, the core of any brick-and-mortar business has always been the relationship between the owner or employees and the customer—that's what drives our business. We're not just punching keys in an office, taking orders, and shipping product. The reason I emphasize this is because if you want to succeed with a brick-and-mortar business, you have to actually like interacting with people. If you don't have a passion for helping and serving people, don't bother.

What kind of business should you start? For me, it was a pawn shop. Due to my experience, training, and interests, there was no question. What's your thing? What do you know better than anyone else?

A Latin saying I always tell my employees is *Temet Nosce*, which means "Know thyself."

When you open a business, you have to know your own personal passions, strengths, and weaknesses. Don't focus on what's going to make you the most money; money should be a byproduct of opening a business you're passionate about. Focus instead on what you're best at, what you'll love doing the most, because if you're successful, this is what you're going to be doing for the rest of your life. If you can cook, if you're passionate about cooking, open a restaurant. Don't open a jewelry store because you think there's more money in diamonds. Never chase the money—chase the passion.

LeBron James plays basketball. He doesn't run a landscaping business. He knows what he's good at. Do the same. If you try to open a business that doesn't match your strengths and passion, you set yourself up for failure.

OPENING IS THE EASY PART

Anyone can open a business today. It's easy. You open an account, put some money in the bank, and go to the commissioner of revenue and get a business license. Then, you lease a storefront, and you're ready to go. That's the easy part. However, are you aware that 80 percent of all small businesses in the US fail within a year? (Honestly, from my own experience, I'm surprised it's not higher than that.)

You see, opening a business might be easy, but running a successful business is incredibly hard. I know—I've done it multiple times. It's tough as nails. Competition is nasty. Everyone looks out for themselves, and competitors are always trying to undermine you. Your employees might screw you over. Nobody will hold your hand and tell you it's going to be okay, so you'd better have the strength within yourself. If not, you'll quickly find yourself falling into that 80 percent.

That sounds scary, but it doesn't have to be. If you feel motivated to open a business, you owe it to yourself to try, even if you wind up failing. You can always go and get a normal nine-to-five job if things don't work out. In my opinion, the worst thing is not trying. What if I had sat in my house that first night and said, "I don't think I can do it. I'll go sell cars instead?" If I'd gone down to the Ford dealership and gotten a job, I would have regretted it. If I'd wound up selling cars instead of opening a business, I might have made a decent living, but someday, when I reached sixty-five or seventy, I would have looked back and wished I hadn't given up. That regret would have been a nightmare for me. If opening a business is your dream, it's better to give it a shot and fail than give up.

The good news is, if you have a good idea or product, and you're willing to work your ass off, there's a market out there for almost anything. If coffee is your thing, there's a market for coffee that can make you millions of dollars. If you love to design clothes, you can make millions off clothes. Wherever you are right now, look around you. Every single item in the room around you, no matter what it is, began as a dream in the mind of someone who worked hard to turn it into a reality, and they probably made a lot of money doing it.

HOW HARD IS IT?

Once your business is up and running, it's a matter of working as hard as you can. That's easier said than done, and it requires a pretty big transformation in your life. When you leave a normal job to start your own business, you no longer have a manager telling you what to do. You no longer have a boss keeping you accountable and making sure you do the right thing. You are your own boss and your own manager. You are everything, the alpha and omega and everything in between for your business. Everything is on you.

In the early days of my business, I found that liberating and exciting, but also very, very difficult. It takes a lot of getting used to. Since you have no boss, you have to constantly motivate yourself to get everything done. You have to make yourself work hard every single day. I found myself working in the store over sixty hours a week for the first three years before I ever hired a single employee. Like I said before, that only includes the hours I was physically in the store. That doesn't take into account all of the mental work I did when I was away from the store. In fact, I'd say all the hours of mental work, of racking my brain to think of ways to improve my business, were harder and more exhausting than the physical work.

Combining the two, I'd say I easily worked eighty or ninety hours a week. I would get personal phone calls at home at night, and I'd answer with my business name—it was just ingrained into me. Americans love a get-rich-quick scheme, but those opportunities are few and far between. Ninety-nine percent of all successful business owners get there by working their asses off for a long time. The only thing you can control completely is how hard you work, and if you want great results, you have to put in the hours. You will only get out what you put in.

If you're like me, your business is your one-and-only chance to make it work. If I had failed with my first business—and I came close—I would have had to pack it up and get a regular job for the rest of my life. No education means no other way of obtaining capital. If I'd failed, nobody else would have taken a chance on me. Making that first store succeed was my only option, and it motivated me to work as hard as I possibly could.

STICK-TO-ITIVENESS

Perseverance, tenacity, and resiliency—these are the qualities you must exhibit in order to make it. I always wrap them up in a single word: stick-to-itiveness. It's a word they love to use on ESPN. Your business journey is never a straight line. It's never as simple as going from point A to point B. It's a rollercoaster, with ups and downs, peaks and valley. Things might be good for a while and then suddenly take a turn for the worse. You have to be ready to navigate all the different scenarios you will face, whether you're doing well or not doing well. You have to be in it for the long haul, because the road is unpredictable.

There will be times when you're not making as much money as you want, when it seems like you're not making any progress, and you want to quit. How you handle the difficult times determines whether you pull through and become successful or wind up working double shifts at the local UPS store. Which do you prefer?

Having said that, I did sincerely think about quitting one time. Eight months into opening my store, when I was still struggling to get by, I experienced an incident that almost made me give up. At that point, the bills were getting paid, and I was building a healthy customer base. I talked to everyone who walked through the door, got to know them, and worked hard to build relationships that would last for years. For the first time, I started to get excited about the future. Things were headed in the right direction, even though my then-fiancée and I shared that old Toyota.

The day it all went to hell started out as a normal day. Like every other morning, my fiancée dropped me off at work and went about her business. She was working and going to school at the same time. I got out of the car, unlocked the front door of the shop, and immediately knew something was wrong—things were out of place. Items were on the floor that didn't belong there. I walked to the back of the store, turned on the lights, and discovered that someone had broken in.

It was bad—really bad. It looked like multiple people had done it. Somehow, they'd bypassed our alarm system, which meant they'd had free rein of the entire place for however long they wanted.

The jewelry showcases were completely empty. Every piece of gold or silver had been stolen, and those were our main commodities. I walked to the back room and discovered that our safe was wide open and empty. All of the cash was gone. Most importantly, every single piece of pledged gold or silver that I'd stored in the safe was gone. What "pledged" means is that those items belonged to my customers. In the pawn industry, we loan a certain amount of money based on an item's value, and the customer has a certain amount of time to come back, repay the loan with interest, and pick up whatever item they left. All of those items were gone, hundreds of pledged items worth over $100,000 in total.

To make matters worse, I didn't have business insurance at the time. It was one expense I thought I could skimp on—I was wrong. Luckily, every pawn shop contract has a bunch of legal print that says the business is not responsible for merchandise destroyed by an act of God or stolen during a break-in, so technically, I didn't have to replace any of the pledged items. I could have gone that route, but that would have alienated every one of my customers, and they would never have done business with me again.

I wasn't rolling in money at that point, but I had worked hard to build a solid foundation and develop good relationships with all of my customers. I knew many of them on a first-name basis, I knew their families, and all of that was in jeopardy if I didn't make things right. I knew, even then, that how I handled the situation would ultimately determine where my business went. If I stuck to the contract and defended my legal rights, I would have killed my momentum.

I could have apologized to my customers and told them I didn't have insurance to cover the loss, but I didn't do that either. If I was going to fail at my business, it wasn't going to happen like that. So, I decided that in the following weeks and months, I would meet with every single customer who had lost a pledged item—we're talking about hundreds of people. Every time one of them came through the door, I pulled them aside and explained what happened. Even though we didn't have to replace the stolen items, I took responsibility and made it right with every single person. I had so many uncomfortable conversations over the course of a few weeks, but I persevered.

Making it right created a two-sided problem. First, I had to come to a satisfactory agreement with each customer about the monetary value of the stolen item. That was tricky, because a lot of the jewelry had sentimental value, so I had to find an amount that satisfied the customer. Second, I had to convince them that they could still trust me, that it was still safe to do business with me for years to come. Thankfully, I can tell you that most of them still do.

Most of the customers who lost items during that break-in still do business with us because of the way I handled it. I went above and beyond to settle with each and every one of them, making sure that they were not only monetarily satisfied, but reassured about working with me. I chose to be honest and up-front, and I promised each customer that we would invest heavily in safer storage, better security measures, and good, solid business insurance.

When all was said and done, I had gone from being

excited about the direction of my business to being on the verge of bankruptcy. Can you imagine what that feels like? Not only had I left a full-time job and regular paycheck, but I'd poured almost a year of hard work into my business. Just about the time things had begun to go well, I had to start all over again. I could have quit. Maybe it would have been the smarter decision at the time, but I knew the regret would have been worse. In the end, I stuck with it, and that horrible experience made me better and smarter.

GETTING PUNCHED IN THE FACE

That period of time was my worst experience as a business owner, but when you're an entrepreneur, it's a lot like being a boxer. Sometimes you're going to get punched in the face—it's bound to happen. It might be a small punch, or it might be a haymaker. When you get hit, you have two options: get back up and move forward, or give up. If you have the will to persevere during the storms, during the really bad times, it can reinforce your focus and help you become a stronger person. By forcing me to confront a problem head-on, that terrible experience taught me a lot.

Steve Jobs famously said, "I'm convinced that about half of what separates the successful entrepreneurs from the non-successful ones is pure perseverance."

I love that quote, and it's so true. If you keep your head down and keep pushing forward, things will work out, even in the worst of times. When something devastating happens, you can get through it. I failed by not having better security and not having business insurance, but that kind of failure is only the end of your business if you quit. Look, I've failed many times in business. I've hired the wrong people. I've tried new things that didn't work. It will happen to you, too. As long as you learn from those mistakes, then they aren't really failures, because they're helping you to become better.

LEARNING FROM HOT DOGS

Patience is a virtue that goes hand-in-hand with persever-ance. It's hard not to want immediate success in business, but I can't stress enough how important it is to be patient, especially in a new business. You aren't going to be killing it within a month. You won't instantly make a six-figure income, no matter what you've heard on Facebook from these people trying to sell real estate programs. You must be patient. It's not a sprint, but a marathon. That's a cliché, but it's absolutely true.

Too many people read stories about developers creating apps or websites and then selling them after a year for billions of dollars, and they buy into it. Those kinds of things happen to, maybe .0001 percent of people, so it's mostly bullshit. The only people who experience overnight success are people who win the lottery.

You don't have to be in a hurry. Too many people get into business trying to impress their friends, or to make Mom and Dad proud, so they push too fast and too hard. When they don't find success right away, they throw in the towel. It takes time, so try to sit back and enjoy the day. Enjoy the grind, the hard work. Enjoy pouring everything you have into the business. Enjoy meeting with people, developing relationships, learning and honing your craft, and laying a strong foundation that will eventually pay off. Don't worry about next week or next month.

I learned this from the example of Raymond. I met him before I started my own business, when I worked at the old pawn shop. He was already in his seventies, and he liked to come by the pawn shop, because we had a whole wall of compact discs for sale. He collected CDs, so he'd shuffle in once or twice a week to see what we had. Raymond always wore cardigan vests. He was a super nice guy, down-to-earth and funny.

Over time, he shared his story with us. Raymond had owned and operated a small local restaurant for forty years before he sold it and retired in comfort and ease. The restaurant he'd owned was tiny, with no seating of any kind and a very limited menu. All it had was a few parking spaces and a walk-up window. You walked up to the window, placed your order, and got a number. Then, you waited for them to call your number, picked up your food, and ate it in your car.

I couldn't understand how Raymond had made so much money from this tiny little restaurant that only sold hot dogs, hamburgers, and French fries. Finally, I asked him, and the answer he gave me was the simplest answer ever, but it wound up becoming one of the most important pieces of advice that anybody has ever given me.

"I just focused on selling hot dogs every day, and the money took care of itself."

For years, this man went to work selling God knows how many hot dogs, three for a dollar, but he was patient, he paid attention to details, and he won the game on a day-by-day basis. It paid off for him. I took that advice with me when I opened my first store.

I didn't start out with a goal of opening multiple stores or having thirty employees. My goal was to pay my bills, and I concentrated on every customer that walked through the door and every transaction I made. I didn't dream of becoming a big company. I knew, right down to the dollar, how much I needed to make every day to pay the bills. Some days, I made enough, and some days, I didn't, but I kept going.

If you've ever seen a horse race, you know that the horses wear blinders. The blinders prevent them from seeing anything other than what's right in front of them. That's the kind of focus you need to have. Put your blinders on and go to work. Win today, and the future will take care of itself.

THE STANFORD MARSHMALLOW EXPERIMENT

Years ago, researchers at Stanford performed an experiment on kids to test their willpower. It illustrates something I'm trying to say. They set these kids at a table and made them an offer. The researcher would place a marshmallow on the table and tell the kid, "I'm going to leave the room. While I'm gone, you can eat the marshmallow. But if you wait ten minutes and don't eat it, I will return and give you a second marshmallow."

Basically, the kids had to choose between instant gratification or long-term investment. As you might imagine, most of the kids ate the marshmallow as soon as the researcher left the room, but some kids waited. The kids who waited got two marshmallows. Years later, as a follow-up to the study, they discovered that the kids who had waited for two marshmallows wound up doing better in school and had more successful careers.

So which kind of kid are you?

If you can wait, be patient in your business, maintain your focus and work hard every day, you can have greater success down the road. So, let's take a further look down that road together.

CHAPTER TWO

BUILD TRUST FROM DAY ONE

—

The people who pay for the goods and services on offer form the backbone of any successful business. Whether you think of them as customers, clients, or "Michael who works at the local grocery store," you must build trust with these people in order for your business to thrive and grow. When anyone asks me why I think my company has achieved so much success, or why we stand out from the competition, I always tell them it comes down to the genuine, authentic relationships we develop with our customers. Without those relationships, our business wouldn't survive.

THE STORY OF MRS. WILLIS

Once upon a time, a sweet old lady in her 70s walked into my pawn shop with a handful of jewelry. She stood at a mere four-foot-eight, but she seemed lively and full of energy. From the second she walked through the door, I thought of her as more than a mere transaction. It was the first year of my business, and I'd promised myself that I would always take a few minutes to get to know every single customer.

Immediately, I greeted her, asked how she was doing, and spent some time getting to know her. I learned that her name was Mrs. Willis.

I asked her that all-important question, "How can I help you today?"

Initially, she gave a typical, guarded answer. "I need to pawn some jewelry for a short-term loan."

However, as I engaged her in conversation, she shared with me a bit about her personal life.

"My daughter wants to open her own vitamin store," she said. "I'm hoping I can help her out."

I could tell that, like many first-time customers, Mrs. Willis didn't have a high opinion of the pawn industry. She told me that she'd done business with numerous pawn shops over the years, and she'd never been treated especially well. She came into my store expecting to have to stick up for herself. That's because many pawn shops intentionally try to offer customers as little as they can. They think it makes good business sense to lowball customers; it doesn't. It only antagonizes them and destroys any chance of creating long-term loyalty.

Mrs. Willis assumed I wouldn't loan her all the money she needed to help her daughter, and when she showed me the jewelry, she had a skeptical look on her face. I've seen that look before. She expected to be disappointed.

"How much will you give me for this?" she asked.

Examining the jewelry, I could see roughly how much it was worth. Instead of quoting an amount, I asked her another question.

"How much were you hoping for?"

As it turned out, the amount she hoped for was the exact amount her daughter needed to open her vitamin store. Furthermore, that amount was clearly well above what the jewelry appeared to be worth.

The safest option from a financial perspective would have

been to loan her exactly the amount of money the jewelry was worth. After all, you don't give people more than you owe them, right? You don't pay customers extra money out of the kindness of your heart, do you? That doesn't make sense.

However, I had set a goal, and I believed in it. I intended to provide meaningful help to every single one of my customers, and when I heard Mrs. Willis's story, I made up my mind to provide the best customer service I could. To her surprise, I told her I would loan her the exact amount she needed to help her daughter. I took a risk in doing that, of course, but something in my gut told me that Mrs. Willis would appreciate it. She'd gotten average or below-average service at other pawn shops. By going above and beyond, I hoped she would come back, pay her loan, pick up the jewelry, and quite possibly, go on to become a loyal customer.

"I hope that helps." I added, "Tell your daughter I wish her good luck with her vitamin business. I hope everything works out."

She thanked me and went on her way. By the time she left the store, her whole demeanor had changed.

My risk enabled her daughter to open the vitamin store, but that was far from the end of our relationship. After the initial loan, and for many years afterward, Mrs. Willis came into my pawn shop a couple of times a week, every week. She liked to check out any jewelry that we had in stock, and she often pawned other items. Sometimes, she came in the store just to see how I was doing. Not only did she become a repeat customer, but she became a genuine friend of mine.

When other people came into the store while she was there, she praised our services and encouraged them to do business with us. She became a walking advertisement for my pawn shop. In fact, I have Mrs. Willis to thank for some of our current customers. One act of above-average customer service created a lifetime of loyalty and promotion. At the same time, I felt good knowing that I'd genuinely helped her daughter start the business of her dreams. Nothing feels better than making a difference while making a living. Word-of-mouth advertising is the best form of advertisement. It's free, but it's also priceless.

GENUINE RELATIONSHIPS

Developing, and more importantly, maintaining genuine relationships with your customers lays a strong foundation for a successful business. A business that treats customers as little more than a source of money hurts itself in the long run. Treat your customers poorly if you want your business to fail—it's as simple as that.

At Riverside Pawn, most of the people we do business with are loyal return customers. All you have to do is show people you care about them on a personal level. When you do that, they don't want to do business anywhere else. We've been in business long enough now that we enjoy second-generation customers as well. We took great care of the parents, and now we get to provide that same excellent service to their grown-up kids. A reputation for customer care gets passed down through families.

Mrs. Willis's daughters do business with our pawn shops, and I maintain the same meaningful relationships with them that I did with their mom. When Mrs. Willis passed away a few years ago, the family invited me to the funeral, and one of her daughters gave me a laminated obituary to remember her by, which I keep on my desk in my home office to this day. This means far more to me than a large profit margin ever could.

APPRECIATE EXISTING CUSTOMERS

Too many businesses put all of their focus on acquiring new customers to increase their profits, but the real secret to growth comes from treating existing customers as well as you possibly can. Brick-and-mortar businesses thrive on word-of-mouth advertising, and if you give someone great customer service, they'll want to tell others about you.

If someone likes your shop, and they find out a friend or family member is looking for the products or services you provide, there's a good chance they'll recommend you. That kind of sincere customer recommendation is entirely in your control. If you want people to recommend your business, make them feel appreciated and cared for. Do this consistently, and you'll see the difference. New customers will begin to walk through the door saying, "Hey, my friend told me this was a great business."

These kinds of genuine customer relationships offer more than professional perks. While your business will grow, your career will also feel much more rewarding. I can't tell you how great I feel every day knowing that my job helps people. My whole team gives 100 percent commitment to everyone. We want our customers to feel cared for, but at the same time, we feel great, too. I love it when customers bring their babies to the store to introduce them to me.

I used to look forward to seeing Mrs. Willis every week over those eight or nine years. At this stage in the business, I'm no longer on the front line, so I don't get as much of a chance to form one-on-one relationships with customers as I would like. However, I still experience occasional reassuring moments. For example, while I was visiting one of my stores, a long-time customer spotted me and came over to catch up. We chatted for a while. I asked about her husband, who suffers from Parkinson's disease and uses an oxygen tank. This was no feigned concern. I genuinely wanted to know how he was doing. She told me about their latest medical struggles, and I expressed sympathy.

The next time I saw her, she came into the store with her husband. He walked up to me and handed me a hand-drawn portrait of superheroes with our company logo in the corner. He knew I liked comic books, and, according to his wife, he used drawing and art as a way to cope with his disease. The drawing he gave me looked so elaborate, it must have taken him days to make it.

That kindhearted gesture from a customer meant so much to me. The feeling of making money doesn't even come close to how I feel in a moment like that. It makes every minute of hard work more than worthwhile. When you cultivate meaningful relationships, customers become more than customers. They become part of your extended family, and when that happens, they don't even consider doing business anywhere else. I feel sorry for businesses that only try to take advantage of customers or squeeze every penny out of them. They have no idea what they're missing out on.

EVERY CUSTOMER'S CHOICE

Every customer who walks through your door does so by choice. They picked your business when they could have just as easily gone to another store down the street. As a business owner, it's your job to convince people to choose you over your competition, so think long term. Don't view customers as a single interaction, a single exchange of money, but as people who matter, people you want to know and serve for years to come. Get to know every customer on an individual level and do it for the right reason. Be sincere. Believe it or not, it's very easy to tell when someone is only being nice to you for their own financial gain.

Most business owners understand that they benefit from providing good customer service, but not all of them put it into practice. And not all business owners go far enough. There's no trick to cultivating real relationships with people. It doesn't require secret information or some subtle technique. All you have to do is treat everyone who comes through your door in the best way possible—not just once or twice, but every single time you interact with them, even if they've already been coming in for years.

Think of the customer as your boss. That's what I constantly tell my team. I might have the power to hire and fire employees, but the customer can fire both them and me. If customers turn against us, they can shut down the whole business—that's how it works. I also tell my employees, if they want a promotion, treat every customer the way they'd treat their boss when trying to get a promotion.

We all have bad days, but a customer doesn't deserve to be burdened with your personal problems. Set your feelings aside when interacting with customers. Anybody can give great customer service when they're in a great mood, but the people who are best at it give great customer service no matter what's going on in their personal lives.

CONVERSATIONS OVER TRANSACTIONS

Every time a customer walks into your store, you have a chance to create a positive impression of yourself and your business, but you also have the opportunity to get to know them as a person. My team understands the value of conversations over transactions. When you walk into Walmart and the greeter gives you a robotic, "Hello, how are you today?" or when the cashier says, "Have a nice day," and you know they don't mean it, how does that make you feel? Does it make you feel valued? Does it make you want to come back? Of course not. Empty words don't mean much.

Too many customers have had interactions with employees who clearly don't care about their jobs, let alone their customers. These workers do the bare minimum in order to receive their paychecks. They might say the right words, but they look stressed out, tired, and uninterested. Instead, I tell all of my employees to relax, be themselves, and to be sincere. I don't give them a script to memorize, or a line to repeat.

It's human nature to want to form connections with other people based on empathy, not on robotic reactions. Talk to your customers about their hobbies, their interests, their families. We like to joke with them, laugh with them, and express sympathy when appropriate.

Face-to-face communication is crucial. My daughter is eighteen years old, and I worry a little bit about her generation. I worry that they have too much attachment to online relationships at the expense of in-person relationships. With e-commerce, Twitter, Facebook, and Instagram, people spend most of their time on their phones, sharing their lives on social media. They can get so distracted by their online life that they miss out on developing relationships with the people who are right there in front of them. If it happens in their personal lives, it can also happen in their professional lives as well.

I'm forty years old, and when I was growing up, cell phones didn't really exist. We looked people in the eye when we spoke to them, and we said "please" and "thank you." If brick-and-mortar businesses expect to survive in the age of e-commerce, business owners and their employees must develop proper social and interpersonal skills. This is the strength we have over the convenience of e-commerce. If you're a young entrepreneur looking to get ahead in the brick-and-mortar world, recognize the importance of face-to-face communication. Focus on developing genuine relationships with others. You can't run a business like this successfully from behind a computer screen. Make eye contact. Smile. Connect. It's more important than ever.

Keep one thing in mind, most customers who walk into a pawn shop would rather be somewhere else. They come to us because they need a quick loan—maybe to pay their rent or bills, maybe to buy groceries, or possibly to get themselves out of an uncomfortable situation. Our job, then, is to empathize with the hard circumstances of our customers, and to make that difficult transaction as smooth and simple as possible. I personally find it quite easy to empathize with most of my customers, because I've been in their position before. Growing up, we sometimes paid for groceries by pawning my mother's jewelry. Even as a young boy, I understood how important pawn shops were to my family, because we relied on them financially. In fact, the guy who often pawned my mom's jewelry became an accountant and mentored me when I first went into business. I learned so much from him.

Whatever kind of business you own, the principles still apply. Make it your ultimate goal to listen to your customers, understand their needs, and make their lives easier. Your business will benefit greatly in the long run, and you'll feel better about your job.

THE SECOND MOST IMPORTANT RULE

Everyone knows the most important rule of running a business: the customer is always right. Do you know the second most important rule? It goes like this: if you're absolutely positive that the customer is wrong, read the first rule again.

If a customer genuinely seems to be in the wrong, I strongly encourage you to swallow your pride and consider the long-term repercussions of how you respond. If you choose to respond with kindness, rather than insist on your rightness, your customers become far more likely to return and do business with you. That's worth whatever frustration you feel by giving in to their demands. Turn complaints into compliments.

Look at the example of Amazon. If you order an item from Amazon and find it broken upon delivery, all you need to do is contact them and return the item for a refund. Their return policy states that any item that comes from the company can be returned for any reason within thirty days. They make the process easy by providing postage-paid mailing labels, so all you have to do is repack the item, apply the label, and give the package to the postman. They don't fight customers over individual transactions. Do they lose money by doing this? In many cases, probably so. However, they would rather ensure that you continue using their service and ordering from them in the future. Losing a little money on a single transaction doesn't compare to years of customer loyalty. That's why they've developed a reputation for great customer service.

We had a customer pick up a TV she had pawned. A team member helped load it into the customer's vehicle. Two hours later, she called to complain about a big crack in the screen. When I spoke to my team member, he claimed that the TV was in perfect condition when he loaded it. We checked the parking lot CCTV and realized that the customer had cracked the TV screen when she slammed her trunk shut.

At that point, we had two options. First, we could have fought her, told her she'd cracked the TV herself, showed her the CCTV footage, and refused to buy her a new one. Although technically we would have been in the right to do so, things would likely have turned ugly, and we probably would have lost a customer forever. Even if she'd admitted her fault, she would have left the store humiliated. The last thing you want to do is embarrass a customer.

Second, we had the option to simply take care of the problem and buy her a new television. Even though we didn't owe it to her, replacing the broken TV would make her happy and encourage her to continue doing business with us. Of course, that's the option we chose. We didn't argue with her about the cracked screen. Even though we knew we weren't in the wrong, we apologized, bought her a new TV, and wished her well. As a result, she continues to do business with us, and the amount of money we've made from her long-term business amounts to far more than the cost of that television.

When you choose the second way, you might have to eat crow, and you might lose out on a little money in the moment, but it's worth it. Always let the customer think they're right, even when they aren't. I know that's a struggle sometimes, because we all want to defend ourselves.

THE IMPORTANCE OF HONESTY

Never underestimate the importance of honesty and credibility in business. Think of your relationship with your customers as a marriage. You can spend thirty years building trust with a spouse, but it only takes a single act of dishonesty to destroy that trust.

This is especially important for our business, since the entire concept of pawning relies on customers trusting us. We receive items that matter to people, objects with emotional connections and sentimental value. Our customers trust us to hold these items until they make enough money to return for them. Contracts typically last between thirty and ninety days. At any point within that time period, the customer can come and pick up the item, provided they pay back their loan with the added interest. If the customer didn't trust that we would take care of their item, the relationship would fall through.

We place a huge emphasis on honesty in our company, so if we tell a customer we'll do something, we put all of our energy into doing it. If an item is due to be sold on a certain day, but the customer calls and requests us not to sell it because they have money coming in later in the week, we keep the item for them. When we promise to keep a customer's item, no matter what, we stick to it. That gains our customers' trust, and their trust guarantees return business.

MISTAKES ARE MADE

I'm not suggesting we've never made a mistake. Although it's very rare, we've had a few instances where items that we said we would hold accidentally got sold. Mistakes are inevitable. We're all human, after all. What matters more than making a mistake is how you handle it. Don't try to make excuses or, worst of all, blame the customer. Always own up and apologize, and then do whatever it takes to satisfy the customer enough to trust you again.

For example, a few months ago, one of our store managers called about a customer looking to redeem her jewelry. He couldn't find her items in the store safe. After investigating, we learned the terrible truth. When the customer had called asking the store to keep her jewelry a little longer, she'd received a verbal promise that we would. Unfortunately, nothing was written down, so the rest of the staff had no idea. The jewelry had been taken out of the safe, sent to a refinery, and melted down. We had no way to get it back.

Clearly, we were at fault. I had to handle the situation and solve the problem to the best of my ability. I met with the customer, who had always been loyal, and I told her the plain and simple truth. I didn't try to sugarcoat it, make excuses, or justify it. Of course, she was upset, and I let her vent her frustrations at me. Then I apologized and focused on how to fix the situation so she would be able to regain her trust in us.

Ultimately, I just asked her, "What can we do to make this right with you?"

Originally, we'd given her a $400 loan at 10 percent interest, expecting her to pay back $440. When I spoke to her that day, she told me that the actual value of the rings we'd lost was $6,000. Because of my experience dealing with jewelry, I knew that the weight of the rings meant they were worth somewhere between $800 and $1,000. I also knew, however, that this lady was a good customer who had done business with us for three years.

"Considering you paid $6,000, what could we do for you right now that would make this situation better?" I asked.

She decided she wanted us to replace a little more than half of the jewelry, so she asked for $3,500. I don't think she actually expected us to give it to her. She seemed to anticipate a negotiation, but immediately, I went over to the safe and pulled out $3,500. I apologized again and offered to give her the money as long as she agreed to keep doing business with us.

She thanked us, accepted our apology, and took the money. Although this proved to be costly, the money didn't matter. You can always make back money, as long as you keep doing business. What mattered was that we recognized we'd made a mistake, learned from it, and kept a loyal customer. She still does business with us to this day.

You can't avoid every mistake, but you can always stick to your word. In our business, we fix every mistake, even if it's not our fault, even if it means a financial loss. If your customers feel wronged, it's your responsibility to make things right. Let them vent a little bit, if they need to. You'll survive. Then do what you can to correct the problem.

THE HEART OF THE MATTER

Every business owner wants to grow their company, turn

a profit, and build a good reputation. In order to do so, you must begin at the heart of the matter. Your business, like every business, depends on its customers for survival. Show them how grateful you are that they've chosen your business over the competition. Never focus on short-term profit. View every financial transaction as an opportunity to show empathy with a person, not a customer, and you'll form meaningful and long-lasting relationships that will benefit your business far into the future.

Remember, your customers could choose any business—make them choose yours. While most businesses think about what they can get out of customers, we do the reverse. We think about what we can give to them. Don't put your time, energy, and resources into profit. Instead, make a difference to every individual who chooses to do business with you, and the money will follow. There is no shortcut. Your business happens one customer at a time, one transaction at a time, so make every moment count.

CHAPTER THREE

BE DIFFERENT. STAND OUT.

Let's face it: pawn shops have a bad reputation. To stand out against the competition in this industry, I made it my goal to change this perception. Each one of our stores is well-lit, clean, and has friendly employees, just like a high-quality retail store. We have nothing to do with the rude pawnbrokers you see on TV, the surly guys who sit around and smoke cigars and snarl at customers. By changing these stereotypes, we've grown our client base dramatically. Our stores attract the people who never expected to enjoy a pawn shop, but when they come in, they wind up having a nice chat, looking around at all of our tidy shelves, and buying from us.

Every company operates according to its own business philosophy. The first pawn company that I worked for focused almost exclusively on making as much money as possible. While I disagreed with this approach, I was merely an employee—I lacked the power to change anything. When you start your own business, you get to choose the philosophy that will drive your decisions.

Once I had the authority to design my own store, I decided to take a "quantity over quality" approach to money. What I mean by that is, I aimed to have a low-profit margin on each individual customer, with the goal of creating a huge customer base to make up for it. The approach worked in the beginning, and it still works today.

The first store I worked at made money from between ten and fifteen transactions per day. Some of my stores make over a hundred transactions a day. Why do we run things this way? Because when you're trying to make as much money as possible off of a single customer, they can tell. It's obvious when you're squeezing every penny out of someone, and people don't like that feeling. It makes them less likely to return to your business.

On the other hand, when you do everything you can to help a customer regardless of the money, you might have a smaller profit margin on that immediate transaction, but the customer will have a much more positive experience.

CREATE CUSTOMERS FOR LIFE

Treat your customers like family. You wouldn't try to make the largest profit off of a family member. Instead, you'd try to give them the most value for their money. Did you know a small business that opens today has a 97 percent chance of failing within ten years? Long-term success is extremely rare, so if you want to survive, you have to stand out. More than that, you have to create loyal long-term customers.

It's not as hard as it seems. A little politeness goes a long way. Once, while driving between stores, my windshield wiper snapped in half. It was raining at the time, so I had to get it fixed right away. I knew of two different auto repair shops within a short distance from my business, so I went to the closest one.

I parked at the first repair shop and hurried inside. I saw not a single customer anywhere. An older gentleman sat behind the counter, his full attention fixed on a computer screen as he browsed the internet. When I walked through the door, even though I was the only customer in the store, he didn't even look up to greet me. I had to approach the counter to get his attention. I explained to him what had happened with my windshield wiper. His response?

"I'd love to help you, but I'm backed up with customer orders. I won't be able to do anything for the rest of the day."

He gave me a sour look, as if I'd inconvenienced him by trying to become a paying customer. I couldn't believe it. The fact that I had to deal with a broken windshield wiper while driving in the rain made no impact. He expressed no sympathy. I wasn't a person to him, and he went right back to his computer screen, as if he'd immediately forgotten all about me. I stood there for a moment in amazement. He had nothing else to say to me, and I refused to stand around and beg for help.

You can imagine how annoyed I felt walking out of that shop. I felt completely unappreciated and unwanted. Do you think there's any chance I would ever visit their store again? Now, to be fair, that worker might've been having a terrible day. Maybe he was going through a rough time in his personal life, or maybe the company had hired him recently and didn't yet realize how bad he was. Unfortunately, none of those excuses changed the way I felt walking back out into the rain to get in my car, sliding in behind the steering wheel and seeing the broken windshield wiper again. That's why I don't tolerate bad customer service from my employees, and that's why I always tell my people, even if you're having a bad day, don't take it out on customers.

I had no choice but to try the second repair shop, as my problem remained unresolved. As I pulled into the parking lot, I saw numerous other vehicles. That boded well.

When I stepped through the door, the atmosphere inside felt completely different from the first place. I saw at least a dozen customers inside. Despite this fact, the second I walked through the door, the guy behind the counter noticed me, made eye contact, and asked me how I was doing. Then he asked what he could do to help me.

When I explained my situation, he asked for my car key. He didn't want me to have to walk back outside in the rain. He went out, heedless of the rain, got into my car, and drove it into the garage. Then he retrieved a brand new windshield wiper from the back of the store and within five minutes, he'd replaced the broken one.

"What do I owe you?" I asked.

"You know, that wiper only costs about three dollars," he said.

He noticed the logo of the pawn shop on my shirt and pointed at it.

"I'll tell you what," he added, "the next time I come to your pawn shop, give me a good deal, and we'll call it even. Don't worry about the wiper. I'm just glad I could help."

Not only did he fix my problem, but he made me feel appreciated. I left that store in a great mood. It improved the rest of my day. That's the power of good customer service.

From that point on, if anyone asked me for a good auto repair shop, I didn't hesitate to recommend the second one. The excellent customer service distinguished them from their competition. Not only will I return and do business with them any time I need auto repair help, but I will continue to point people in their direction. Their windshield wiper wasn't higher quality than at the first shop, but they created an uplifting customer experience. They also created a devoted customer for life—all at the cost of a three-dollar windshield wiper and a friendly attitude.

BE PROBLEM SOLVERS

I often ask my team members (especially new hires) what they think their job is. Most say, "I'm a pawnbroker" or "I'm a salesperson." While they're not technically wrong, I want them to think of themselves as problem solvers.

Every customer who walks through the door has a problem that needs a solution. When someone walks into a coffee shop, their problem is that they want some coffee. The barista is in charge of solving that problem by getting the customer a fresh cup of coffee. Likewise, my team members are to identify a customer's problem and provide a personalized solution to meet the specific need. Some of our customers, for example, need short-term cash, in which case we'll help pawn an item of theirs. Others come in wanting to buy a TV or jewelry, so we help make that happen.

The key is having the right mindset. You can look at your business as a vehicle for profit, or you can look at it as a problem-solving machine. Choose the latter. The more you give as a business, the more you get in return. Although Riverside Pawn is not a national chain, people recognize our name in the six cities where we have stores. While I don't claim we will ever become as big of a brand as Apple, we're looking to establish a similar dynamic. Apple customers are loyal to Apple products, because the company gives them a reason to be.

CREATE BRAND ADVOCATES

We actively and consistently encourage our customers to become brand advocates. A prime example is our turkey giveaway. This began on the first year we opened our store as a way to give back to our customers. The Wednesday before Thanksgiving, we gift turkeys to our loyal customers. A turkey only costs us fifteen dollars, but it allows us to demonstrate how much we care for the people who choose to do business with us. The first year, we gave away ten turkeys. Now that we've grown, some of our stores give away up to a hundred turkeys. This giveaway has made a real difference in the local community. It's a huge event. Big trucks pull up, we have a long list of names, a crowd of people, and lots of happy faces. We consider it crucial to show appreciation for these people. Without them, our business wouldn't succeed.

The giveaway is a great catalyst for word-of-mouth advertising. The event often receives live media coverage, which helps get the word out about what we do for our customers. More importantly, our participating customers spread the word about our giveaway and, consequently, our company. People love sharing good news. Always keep that in mind when you're trying to generate interest in your business.

To spread the word about your business, start locally. Take advantage of every promotion opportunity, no matter how big or small. Attend local events, give away T-shirts, and donate prizes to raffles. While not the most radical or far-reaching forms of advertisement, every little thing helps.

TAKE ADVANTAGE OF SOCIAL MEDIA

We take full advantage of the digital age to promote our business. Social media and online promotion is extremely effective and cost-efficient. While we used to invest in commercials, billboards, TV ads, and newspapers, those cost quite a bit of money, and we had no guarantee that they reached our target audience.

Now, if we have a motorcycle available at one of our stores, we can upload an ad to Facebook and tweak it based on age, sex, interest, zip codes—practically anything. Not only does this cost us pennies, but it allows us to adopt a more targeted approach to advertising. With social media, you can ensure that you get through to the exact people who are interested in what you have to offer. Online ads are immediate, too. You don't have to wait for a newspaper printing or for commercials to be shown on TV. Social media also encourages interaction, meaning you can talk directly with existing and potential customers.

On the other hand, online interaction isn't always positive; that's just something you have to understand and expect. When you upload an ad to Facebook or any other social media platform, you relinquish full control over your content. Internet trolls often leave negative or irrelevant comments that can harm the validity of your ad.

One of our employees left a safe unlocked and a handgun was shoplifted. We had no choice but to make a police report, giving them a video recording of the person who stole the handgun. The police department uploaded the video onto their website, which was then passed on to the news stations, who shared it all over social media. The comments spiraled out of control. We had people insulting our company, criticizing us for our mistake, saying all kinds of hateful things. It generated bad PR that was harmful to our business. We couldn't do anything to stop it. All we could do was acknowledge the mistake on our own social media pages and promise to do better.

Social media has its downfalls, but because of its cost-effectiveness and the ability to target specific audiences, it remains the most effective advertising approach for brick-and-mortar businesses. Still, to minimize the negative, pay close attention and constantly police your social media presence.

GIVE MORE TO GET MORE

In the end, every business wants to stand out, get noticed, and generate positive word of mouth, and every business has their own way of trying to do this. A coffee shop might, for example, offer a cheaper cup of a coffee or tastier cookies. Riverside Pawn puts all of its effort into providing excellent customer service. We are where we are today due primarily to the way we treat our customers. Along the way, we have also created an attractive social media presence, and we interact continually with our local community. We want to be there for people as much as possible. It works, which is why we recommend it so strongly to you. Ultimately, if you want to beat your competition, you have to give more to get more in return.

PART TWO

THE TEENAGER STAGE

CHAPTER FOUR

HIRE THE RIGHT PEOPLE

Once your business starts to grow, you'll reach a point where you're ready to advance from the "toddler" stage to the "teenager" stage. A teenage business doesn't need your constant attention. You can back off a little bit and let the system take care of itself. You're not completely hands-off, but you can distribute the workload to others, giving yourself more time and freedom for experimentation.

Transitioning to the teenager stage means you're ready to grow your team. Taking this next step isn't easy, but you can only expand your business so much if you keep attempting to do everything by yourself. If you want to keep growing, you need help. Otherwise, the quality of your service suffers. Being unable to serve customers quickly and efficiently, or offer them my undivided attention are among my biggest pet peeves. It also puts my nerves on edge when people have to wait in line, or worse yet, aren't even greeted because employees are busy with other customers.

In fact, seeing customers lined up, forced to wait their turn is what first let me know when it was time for my business to take the next step. Remember, the longer customers have to stand around, waiting for someone to talk to them, waiting for help, the worse their experience, and the less they'll think of your business. You need to have enough people on your team to handle the volume of incoming customers, so that every person walking through the door receives attentive service. That, in turn, generates more interest in your business.

Hiring more employees is a difficult decision for most business owners. When you start a business on your own, all of the risk belongs to the individual. If the business fails, you fail alone. Your family feels the effects, but no one else's livelihood is at stake. Once you bring employees on board, you bear responsibility for their well-being as well. They depend on you to create a stable business. The last thing you want to do is offer someone a job, only to turn around and fire them for lack of money.

YOUR FIRST HIRE

Think carefully about your first hire. It's a big deal, and that first employee sets the tone for your business going forward. Make sure you select the right person. When I finally took the risk to hire help, I knew exactly who I wanted. As I mentioned earlier, growing up, my family didn't have a lot of money. That meant my mother had to work in the fast-food industry throughout my entire childhood. She worked long, hard shifts for dead-end jobs that had no future prospects. Even after I started my pawn shop, she continued to work in fast food.

To rescue her from that line of work, I offered her the first position on my staff. Today, she is the manager of one of my stores. Giving my mom a job she actually enjoys has been one of the proudest moments of my life. Not every hire has been as smooth sailing, however.

The one thing I've learned about hiring people is that I don't like doing it. In fact, it's one of the hardest parts of my job. The whole process feels unnatural. In a job interview setting, the person you see is often not representative of their real selves. Instead, they present their most well-spoken and politically correct sides. They behave differently, saying or doing whatever they think the employer wants. You have no guarantee that the person you meet during the interview will bear any similarity to the person who shows up to work on Monday morning.

No matter what you do, hiring is always a gamble. You never know exactly what sort of new employee you're going to get, even when you do your best during interviews. I've interviewed and hired some of the most intelligent and presentable candidates, people with fantastic experience, who said all the right things. While they seemed excited and ready to work hard, some of them never even showed up to work on their second day. They lasted one shift and gave up. I've had this happen with people I never would have expected it from. It took me completely by surprise.

DON'T JUDGE A BOOK BY ITS COVER

You can't judge a book by its cover. That saying is so very true when it comes to hiring people, and it goes both ways. Some of the most clean-cut, presentable interview subjects turned out to be disappointments, but I've had the opposite experience as well.

Let me tell you about one of the best employees I've ever hired. He's worked for me now for seven years. At first glance, he didn't look very professional. When he first came in, he had messy hair and wore a plain T-shirt and jeans. At eighteen years old, he wasn't well-spoken and had absolutely no work experience. Some of his responses to my interview questions sounded awkward. He didn't have eloquent answers. Does that sound like the kind of person you would take a chance on? But I did. I just had a gut feeling, so I went with it. I now consider him one of the most important members of my team.

As it turns out, this young man has an impeccable work ethic. He puts 100 percent of his effort into every single thing he does. While his commitment and job performance would be impressive for any employee, what makes it more impressive is that this particular individual also has cerebral palsy. His disability makes all physical activity just a little bit harder for him, but he never complains or refuses a task. He could probably receive disability checks, but he chooses not to. Instead, he works hard and provides for himself.

Over the years, he has demonstrated time and again just what a passionate and dedicated worker he is. He treats every customer with the utmost care and attention. Any time I can't deal with a customer personally, which is most of the time these days, I depend on him first and foremost. If I can't solve a problem myself, I trust him to solve it, and he's never let me down.

You can't know for sure the quality of a new hire until you actually see them in practice. How, then, can you possibly make the right decision when hiring people? That's the million-dollar question. Sadly, there's no foolproof guide. I say that after years and years of experience. I tend to go with my instincts. Hiring is trial and error. There is no way to be certain about your decision, so make whatever choice feels right at the time and go from there.

When interviewing a candidate, ask questions beyond merely their work history or what they want out of the job. Get to know the person behind the resume. I like to sit in on interviews to get a sense of my prospective employees. Chiefly, I want to get a sense that I can trust them, which is especially important in my business because, while most modern companies use credit cards and checks, Riverside Pawn is 80 percent cash. That means over $10 million a year flows through the cash drawers of more than thirty employees. Whoever I hire must be trustworthy enough to properly run and maintain those drawers.

FIRING NEVER GETS EASY

Even harder than hiring employees is firing them. Unfortunately, firing people is an inevitable part of becoming a business owner, and it doesn't get any easier the more you do it. I empathize with people who desperately need their jobs—they have bills to pay. In some instances, they have a family to provide for.

I've been in their position. I know they have kids to feed, rent to pay, lives to sustain. I hate letting people go, but sometimes it has to be done. Overall, I consider myself a laid-back boss, and I think my entire team would agree.

I don't fire people on the spot for problems that can be fixed. Tardiness, for example, can be dealt with. When people make mistakes, we work with them to correct the problem.

I recommend not firing people unless it becomes absolutely necessary to do so. Though I'm willing to forgive and work with employees on many issues, I have a few deal breakers, and so should you. If an employee provides bad customer service, or if they are dishonest with me, then they can't work in my company. Why? Because those two issues go to the heart of the whole company. We run our business based on customer service and honesty. Without them, we have nothing. When I see a worker of mine acting rudely to customers, it's best to cut ties and let them go before that attitude rubs off on other employees. Similarly, if an employee is habitually dishonest, it's better not to let them get away with it, because it might negatively influence company culture.

HIRING FAMILY

I mentioned before that my mother was my first hire, but despite this fact, I actually encourage people to think twice before employing family or friends. In total, I have given jobs to nine family members and friends, mostly because I felt a responsibility to help them get on their feet. Of course, you want to help people you care about.

And when you have the means to provide them with steady work, it's tempting to do so.

Out of all of the family and friends I've hired, however, my mom was the only success story. Every other example turned out to be a mistake. I thought I was being a good person, but I didn't consider the long-term implications of mixing business with my personal life. In a few cases, it backfired on me in terrible ways. Since then, I have established a company rule not to hire family or friends, or friends of management. Maintaining a separation between your personal and professional lives provides an important buffer.

Why is that? Because when you work with people you know on a personal level, you tend to treat them differently. The personal relationship bleeds over. Without meaning to, you hold them to a different standard, even if you're doing it subconsciously. For example, you might be inclined to give them more days off, or to deal more gently with their mistakes and poor performance. Employees lose respect for nepotistic leaders, so when you hire friends, you risk demoralizing other people in your team.

It's hard enough to fire regular employees, so having to fire a friend or family only feels that much worse. Not only do you end the working relationship, but you risk damaging and losing the personal relationship too.

After successfully employing my mother, the second family member I hired to work for my company was my cousin. We grew up together and were always very close. Naturally, when I found out he needed a job, I offered him one. How could I refuse to help someone I cared about?

Everything went well for a while, but then I discovered that he was stealing from the company. Some gold jewelry went missing during his shift. Having to confront someone who mattered to me so much felt extremely uncomfortable. My cousin admitted to taking the jewelry, claiming he needed the money to fix his car.

"I'm sorry, man. I was desperate. I just needed the money really bad. It'll never happen again."

I was heartbroken, betrayed by my own family. Someone I thought of as a brother was stealing from me. I fired him on the spot. What choice did I have?

He stopped speaking to me for a long time afterward. He got a new job in another city and worked there for a while, but eventually he had to move back. When he returned, he begged me to give him another chance.

"You can trust me," he said. "I made a mistake, but it won't happen again. Give me one more chance to prove myself. We've known each other so long."

You'd think he would have learned from his mistakes, or I would have learned from mine. I felt sorry for someone I cared about so much. We grew up together. He was practically my brother. I couldn't say "no" to him, so I hired him again.

It didn't take long before more gold jewelry went missing. Once again, he admitted to taking it, and once again, he said he'd done it out of desperation. He apologized. He pleaded with me. He appealed to our close relationship, but I let him go.

Three years have now passed, and we haven't spoken a word to each other. We may never speak again. In firing my cousin, I didn't just lose an employee. I lost one of my best friends. If I could've predicted the damage that hiring him would cause our relationship, I never would've done it. Just because he was a close relative and a good friend didn't mean he had a strong work ethic. I had to learn that the hard way, sadly.

Another time, I hired the wife of a close friend of mine. The position started off as part-time work, but it needed to grow as the company grew. Unfortunately, through no fault of her own, my friend's wife struggled to keep up with the increasing responsibilities. She had four kids, and she knew she couldn't provide what the position needed as we grew. Things became so strained that she finally quit, but it impacted my friendship with her husband for a while.

Eventually, we patched things up, and we're friends again. But it wasn't worth the strain and stress. That's why I strongly recommend that you avoid working with friends and family. When there's strain, it follows you into your personal life—you can't avoid it. After all, the business world is far from fair, and as an owner, your priority must be protecting your business. When you make a decision in the interest of the business, it too often causes conflict with personal relationships. It's just not worth it.

SET BOUNDARIES

Take the time to set healthy boundaries between you and your team members. When you hire people, you're signing up to spend around eight hours a day with them. It's natural that you'll start to like people you spend that much time with. Be careful, however, when crossing the line between a working relationship and a personal one.

A few years ago, I hired a guy I didn't know beforehand. Not only was he a good employee, but we got on well outside of work. We eventually became good friends, hanging out and going to sporting events together. Everything went well until he had a promotion opportunity at work. Out of all the options, I didn't consider him the right person for the promotion, so I chose someone else. It was purely a business decision, but he took it personally.

"How could you do this to me?" he said. "I thought we were friends!"

I tried to explain my reasoning, but he quit right then and there. Soon after, he moved away and got another job. Our friendship had gotten in the way of us working well together, jeopardizing the company.

Now, he is back at Riverside Pawn and works as an assistant manager. We sat down and had a conversation about what happened and how we could avoid similar situations in the future. I am a big believer in direct communication. He expressed that his feelings were hurt, so we decided to lay out the ground rules and set boundaries. I told him I couldn't let myself show favoritism at work, even with a good friend.

Ultimately, you have to prioritize your business, and that means making the best professional decisions, not the best personal ones. Set boundaries between yourself and your employees early on, and communicate them in a clear and effective way to keep your work life separate from your personal life.

TRUST YOUR INSTINCTS

To take your business to the next level, you need to hire an efficient and hardworking team. While it isn't easy to know who to trust, your instincts have gotten you this far—keep trusting them. Listen to your gut when interviewing people, but avoid employing friends and family, as personal relationships can jeopardize a good work environment.

In brick-and-mortar businesses, your staff are on the front line. Choose the right people and make sure to give them the tools they need to succeed and reflect what your company is all about. Doing that requires leadership skills. Just because you can start a business doesn't mean you can lead a team, so that's what we'll look at next.

CHAPTER FIVE

BECOME A LEADER

———

Hiring a team is only the first step. Next, you need to learn how to lead that team. When I first started hiring people, I was in my late twenties. As I mentioned, my first hire was my mother. My second hire, however, was a man in his forties. Not only did I transition to becoming a leader, but I had to lead people older than me, people who didn't necessarily look at me as a leader in other contexts.

When you open a business, you play every role. You are the owner, manager, and employee all at once. When you finally start leading other people, you have to adopt some new qualities, and they don't always come naturally, or easily.

It might sound obvious, but the best way to lead is by example. Actions speak louder than words. Your team members look to you for guidance, so give them something to look at. I value customer service, and I want my team to do the same. To model that value, I go out of my way to form genuine and meaningful relationships with customers.

While I could sit my employees down and explain the value of building these relationships, they learn the lesson in a much more effective way when they see me putting it into practice. As a leader, you create your company culture and become the standard against which your employees will measure themselves. Since customer service lies at the core of Riverside Pawn, I make it my job to show my employees how this culture looks and operates in practice.

CONTROL YOUR EGO

Nothing creates a worse working environment than a leader with an out-of-control ego. We all have a bit of an ego, but I make a point of leaving mine at the door to the office and not bringing it into work with me. Often, when people run businesses, they think they know everything, and they make sure to remind their employees on a regular basis. I don't know everything, and I don't pretend like I do. Pretending doesn't help anyone, and it doesn't contribute to a healthy, thriving business environment.

We should all be working, learning, and improving on

a daily basis. I encourage my team to attend industry conferences and pawn conventions with me so we can learn together. We go to classes and talk to experts about jewelry, diamonds, and firearms. Afterwards, we debrief and share what we've learned.

Every day provides an opportunity to do better, be better, and learn better business skills. I remind myself of this constantly, because I'm the human example of what I want my company to be. If I get lazy, arrogant, or complacent, that attitude will seep into my entire team. Every person you meet can teach you something new. I don't just learn from gun or jewelry experts, but from my team members. I make a point of listening to what they have to say and implementing their best ideas. What sort of business owner would I be if I refused suggestions from my own employees? I know some leaders operate that way, but I don't think any good comes from it.

KNOW WHEN TO PRAISE AND WHEN TO PUNISH

If you want to become an effective leader, you must learn to communicate with your team members. This doesn't just mean giving clear instructions and delegating tasks, although both of those are necessary. Leaders should know every member of their team well enough to understand which style of leadership works best for each individual. I like to remind myself of the carrot-and-stick philosophy. Knowing when to praise and when to punish your employees is key.

Imagine a situation in which two employees have made the same mistake. How should I handle it? Should I approach both employees and scold them? As it turns out, they each react differently. When I speak sharply to employee A, he feels motivated by it, and he works harder as a result. He wants to prove to me that he can meet my expectations. Employee B, on the other hand, feels demotivated by yelling or a confrontational approach. It makes her feel like giving up, and for a few hours after I've yelled at her, she shies away from doing her work, because she's scared to make another mistake. She doesn't want to get scolded again. Employee B, it turns out, reacts better to a calmer, more encouraging approach. The best response for that individual is reminding her gently but firmly, that every mistake creates a learning opportunity. Then I can help her create a practical plan to move forward.

The balance is tricky. Strangely, employee A responds poorly to too much praise and encouragement. If I approach him and tell him he's doing a great job, he actually performs worse. With no real challenge, no way to grow, and nothing to improve, he loses some of his drive to excel.

As you get to know your employees, try to determine

which ones respond better to a firmer hand and which ones require a gentler touch; which ones learn best from punishment and which ones learn best from praise. By leading according to the individual, you get the most out of your team.

I'll share an example. A few years ago, one of my managers made a big mistake. A lot of scamming takes place in the pawning industry, so we have to be careful any time we're dealing with costly items. Often, customers come into stores trying to sell fake diamonds or gold. In this particular instance, a person came in with $7,000 worth of alleged gold bracelets. All of them ended up being fake. Although the manager had tested the bracelets to see if they were real gold, they were such high-quality replicas that they tested positive. Instead of double-checking, he paid the customer what he thought they were worth, and we lost a bunch of money.

When we eventually discovered the gold was fake, I had two choices. Obviously, I could have yelled at and fired the manager. However, I was unwilling to do that because he was a key player in our company. I don't have it in me to fire an employee for an honest mistake, so I turned the situation into a learning opportunity. We had talks, created a practical plan of action to deal with similar situations in the future, and that manager remains with the company to this day.

DON'T HOLD BACK

A leader who effectively communicates with their team members can turn mistakes into vital lessons. These lessons often extend outside of the business world. Every time we hire someone, we teach them not only about good customer service, but everything it takes to work in a customer-centered business. They learn how to become better employees, and along the way, they learn valuable social skills that benefit them in their personal lives. We don't hold anything back—that's big for us. If we have access to tools, resources, or information that can improve our team's professional and personal lives, we make them available.

While that might sound obvious, you'd be surprised at the number of leaders who hold back. Why would they do that? Chiefly, out of fear. Some employers worry that if they give their employees too many tools, and teach them too much, it might backfire if an employee quits and goes to work for a competitor. The way I see it, this is an unfair deal. My employees trusted me by agreeing to work for my company and buying into its culture, so I owe it to them to provide all the tools I can for them to become the best versions of themselves.

You can't expect things to always go well. Focus on staying positive when they don't. The fake gold fiasco, for example, was a bad situation. When faced with such circumstances, there are two typical reactions. The first is negative. You can get angry about losing so much money and make the employee feel horrible about themselves. The second is much more positive, which is the approach I tend to adopt. Not only do I want my employees to see bad situations as learning opportunities, but I want to use them as my own teaching opportunities.

The way you react to a situation flows down and influences the way your team reacts. I want to show my team that negative situations do happen, but they can be handled. Even the biggest problems can be dealt with constructively. Remember that people are listening to your voice. Make it a voice of positivity, hope, and purpose.

THE IMPORTANCE OF PEOPLE

The business world is all about forming relationships. The stronger the relationship between a leader and their team, the stronger the business as a whole. Running a business is a 24/7 job. While it might seem like there aren't enough hours in the day, it's important to find the time to talk to your employees. You need to earn respect from your team members. More than simply leading them, you need to give them a reason to follow you.

I make an effort to stop by all of my stores regularly, both to give my team members a chance to voice any concerns they might have, as well as to get to know them better. I want to know about their personal lives. I want to know their backgrounds, whether they have children or pets or where they would love to travel. We organize events, retreats, and dinners throughout the year where the entire team can come together and hang out.

A business isn't a business without people, and that statement extends beyond customers. The people you employ directly correlate to how successful your business will be. When Riverside Pawn began opening multiple stores, I couldn't be everywhere at once, so I wasn't personally available to help every customer who walked through our doors. My team handles all of those customers in my place, and I trust them to reflect my values with every interaction.

Because they do such a great job, I want them to know how grateful I am. After all, every employee wants to feel rewarded for doing a good job. I do everything in my power to demonstrate that I care about every single person I've hired, making sure they feel comfortable and motivated on both a professional and personal level.

We had a team member who demonstrated all the right qualities. He was honest, dependable, and trustworthy—a good employee. At one point, he began experiencing a toothache, and he wound up having surgery. Afterward, he was prescribed strong painkillers, which allowed him to come back to work. Sadly, his productivity at work decreased, and it became clear that something was wrong.

Since I value face-to-face communication, I sat down and had a conversation with the employee in question. I found out that he had become addicted to his painkillers. In that moment, it would have been easy to fire him. Actually, it would have caused me much less hassle and would have improved the productivity of the company. However, I cared about this person and wanted him to get the proper help. We paid for him to go to a clinic so he could kick his addiction. They weaned him off the drug over a matter of weeks.

After his recovery, that employee wound up leaving our company and going to work for the competition. I imagine many business owners in my position would have felt betrayed. They would have regretted going out of their way to help that person in the first place. I didn't regret it, however, even if he wound up working for a competing pawn shop. It gave me an opportunity to model compassionate leadership to the rest of my team, and, on a personal level, it helped that individual. As I said, I don't hold back any tools I can provide to help an employee in their professional or personal lives.

CREATING COMPANY CULTURE

A leader creates their company culture. The employees who buy into this culture want to be shown what it means to fully embrace it. You set the tone. If customer service is as important to you as it is to me, demonstrate what that means. Learn, learn, and learn some more, so that you improve your own performance along the way. Everyone around you has something new to teach you. Listen to employees, go to classes, attend events in your industry, read books. In the business world, you always have some new tactic, technique, or idea to learn, especially in such a dynamic and ever-changing society.

Think of your team as an investment. The more you give them, the more you get back. Don't hide tools or opportunities. Let them take advantage of everything you have to offer. Being a leader doesn't always come naturally, and being a good leader takes time. Practice makes you better, but remember there is always room for improvement.

If you need more guidance on how to become a better leader, the movie *Boiler Room* offers some excellent advice. There's a scene in which the founder of a brokerage firm (played by Ben Affleck), gives a pep talk to his new recruits.

He says, "There's an important phrase that we use here, and I think it's time you all learned it. 'Act as if.' Do you understand what that means? Act as if you are the fucking president of this firm. Act as if you have a nine-inch cock. Act as if."

Perhaps it sounds a bit extreme, but it makes an important point. Even if I don't know exactly what I'm doing, even if I'm sometimes nervous or uncertain, I try to act confident, positive, enthusiastic, and passionate, so those same qualities can be passed down and reflected back at me by my team.

CHAPTER SIX

STAY ABREAST OF THE COMPETITION

I don't know a single business that doesn't have to deal with competition. Though competition can feel frustrating, and many people perceive it negatively, it's not a bad thing. In fact, it can do wonders for your business, as long as you use it as motivation to work harder and become better.

All competition is not the same. In some of the cities where we operate, we compete with small, local businesses. In many of our other locales, we are up against large-scale corporate stores. Our biggest competition is a mega-corporation that owns over one thousand of the two thousand pawn shops in the United States. Oftentimes, large chains span their profit margins across stores, which can be hard to compete with. The point is, I've dealt with competition of every kind, and I don't mind it. In fact, sometimes I inadvertently create my own competition.

I started my business twelve years ago. At the time, I had a close friend—we'll call him John—who routinely came into the store to hang out. Although I hadn't actually given him a job and didn't pay him, he spent a lot of time waiting on customers and helping me with various tasks. He seemed to enjoy it. In the process, he learned the ins and outs of the pawn industry and, specifically, how my company did business.

A couple of years later, John came to me with an idea. He'd learned about an empty building on the other side of town, and he wanted us to lease it together. He suggested we become partners and open a second store for the business. The property was in a good location, but I decided not to lease it for two reasons. First, I didn't feel ready to expand. Second, when I did expand, I wanted my next store to be located in a different city, so I could reach a brand new market. John understood, and we didn't speak about it again.

Everything seemed fine until a month later, when I got news that the building had been leased and was being converted into a pawn shop. Naturally, I called John to ask him about it. He told me he'd found someone willing to invest money in the property. Together, they intended to open up a store. Initially, I was upset, and I think I had a right to be. My good friend had gotten a deep look behind the scenes at the way I ran my store. He'd taken all the information I'd given him, and he was using it to start his own competing business in the same town.

The situation damaged my relationship with John. However, instead of dwelling on it or feeling sorry for myself, I decided to focus all of my energy on my own business. I held a meeting with the few employees I had at the time and told them about the new competitor. We decided that to stay on top of our game, we would simply keep doing all the things that had worked so well for us over the years, but we would kick everything up a notch. Customer service had always been important, but we made it even more of a priority. We didn't worry about how John's store was doing. We concentrated on becoming the best business we could be.

DON'T OBSESS OVER YOUR COMPETITION

It's very easy to obsess over your competition. However, every minute you spend trying to find out what they're doing is a minute you could have spent improving yourself and your company. I use the racehorse example with my team. As I mentioned before, when a racehorse is in its stall and ready to race, they put blinders on it. That way, the horse doesn't see what's going on around it. It's not looking at the other horses. Instead, it keeps all of its focus on what lies ahead. I recommended taking the same approach in business.

Having said that, as a business owner, I do have some sense of how my competition is doing. Either I hear about them through the grapevine, or I can tell by changes in our own numbers. Don't stay out of the loop entirely. It can help you to know, for example, if your competitors are running promotions or advertisements. At the time, I knew that John's store was doing well enough to remain open—an impressive feat in this industry—but I also knew he didn't pose a real threat to us.

Four years after John's store opened, I heard rumors that it might be up for sale. That's when I took action. I called the owner, John's partner, and introduced myself. We had a friendly conversation, and he told me they were looking for someone to buy out the store. I expressed interest, and he said he'd love to meet with me. At that point, my company already had six locations, but we were ready to open a new store. Riverside Pawn had experienced tremendous success in that particular city. In fact, we did our top numbers there, so two stores in the same town now made sense. I thought opening up a second store would help us to serve even more people in the area.

It was an opportunity I couldn't miss. I bought out the store. Later on, I met with John and told him I wasn't mad at him; I was just doing what I had to do for my business. Fortunately, he understood. Now, John works as a local real estate agent, and he recently helped me buy a property to use as an office.

DOG EAT DOG

On my son's T-ball team, everybody gets a participation trophy. It doesn't matter if they win or lose. It doesn't matter if a specific player performed terribly. Everyone gets a trophy, because we want the kids to feel good about playing. They're only little kids, after all, and they're just learning the basics. Even if they lose every game throughout the entire season, we celebrate and congratulate them at the end.

Business doesn't work that way. The business world can be a selfish place. Everyone is just trying to make a living and get ahead, so it can be "dog eat dog." Friendly competition doesn't truly exist, because there are always winners and losers. Some people do better than others. When one business rises, another falls. That's the way it works, so it's best to accept it and not hold grudges.

I had no idea that letting my good friend John come by the store every week would create competition down the line. My friendship blinded me to the possibility that I was teaching him techniques that might help him steal my customers. No matter where your competitors come from, however, you have to be ready to deal with it. View it as an opportunity to reevaluate the way you do business.

The longer you do business, the more experienced you'll become at dealing with competition. When I left the first pawn shop I worked for, I trained another friend to take over my role. A few years later, he suggested we open a store together. By that point, I had two stores, and I was open to the idea of taking on a partner. My friend and I visited another city together and looked at real estate. Unfortunately, we struggled to put together concrete plans for opening a store together. Though the original idea had been my friend's, he began to drag his feet.

As the process wore on, he became more and more nervous about working with a partner. One day, he called me and said he'd changed his mind; he didn't want to be partners anymore. Instead, he intended to open his own store. That store wound up in the same city as our first store. Once again, I had given birth to my own competition. Again, however, I didn't take it personally. I dealt with it by focusing on the quality of my customer service.

Nowadays, any time we get a new competitor, our business

actually increases. In one of our cities, there are twenty other pawn shops. Because we focus on becoming the best version of ourselves, not only do we do better than our competition, but we do better than we would if we didn't have any.

It isn't my goal to put competitors out of business. However, Riverside Pawn has changed the culture of pawn shops in the cities where we operate. We have set a new standard, which is more modern and respectable than traditional pawn shops. Eight of our competitors have closed in the past three years. Many of these were the stereotypical dark and dingy stores that people imagine when they think of pawn shops.

To thrive, a successful business must evolve along with society. We constantly rethink our strategies and implement new policies that help us stay ahead. Dealing with competition can be stressful, especially when it feels like people are stealing your ideas. When you change the culture of an industry, competitors will inevitably copy your business model. When people see someone achieving success, they want to do the same.

There's no way to prevent that from happening. You don't have control over what other people are doing. What you can control is your own business model, so keep improving it, stay ahead of the copycats. Personally, I like the idea of having others working against me, because it forces me to work harder every day.

CONTINUE GROWING AND EVOLVING

Competition challenges you to continue growing and evolving your business. It forces you to face your weaknesses and eliminate them. Some of the best business decisions are made from outside of your comfort zone. Think of competition as a fire. If you keep it under control, it can be used as fuel. When it heats up, it drives you forward. On the other hand, if it gets out of hand, it becomes uncontrollable and might burn everything around you. Let your competitors motivate you, but don't lose control and let your business go up in flames because of it. That happens when you obsess too much over your competition, when you worry, pace, and lose your temper because someone is challenging you.

Knowing that we have people working against us stops us from being complacent. When you become successful, it can be quite easy to settle. However, as you slow down, others will speed up. If you don't want to be beaten by the businesses around you, stay on top of your game. Don't lose your enthusiasm and don't lose focus.

Competitors can increase awareness about your industry. In the pawn business, for example, having more competition means more pawn shops are opening. That, in turn, means our industry gets more exposure and we get a greater chance to teach people about the quality services we provide. If a town has one pawn shop, many people will likely ignore it. They might not even drive past it. If there are twenty, however, people assume that we must be doing some good, so they're more inclined to come in and see the store for themselves. As soon as they walk through the door, we jump on the opportunity to form a relationship with them. In that sense, competition benefits everyone, as it makes your industry more visible and gives you access to a larger client base.

COMPETITION IS AN OPPORTUNITY, NOT AN OBSTACLE

I know competition can be intimidating. Many people shy away from it, get stressed out by it, or obsess over what everyone around them is doing. I say embrace it. I want my team to look at competition as an opportunity, not an obstacle. Competition shouldn't hinder what you're doing; it should motivate you to do better and be better. A stagnant business will fail. You constantly need to rethink and update your strategies anyway, and competition forces you to do that.

I don't even think of us as competing with others. We are the ones who set the standard, so everyone else is competing with us. The numbers tell me this. In every location where we've opened stores, we have generated more transactions than the other pawn shops around us. Why? Because, whenever we are threatened by a competitor, we focus on ourselves, not on them. We work on becoming the best possible version of ourselves.

Part of becoming the best involves creating a solid, dependable team around you, so next, we'll take a look at building your inner circle.

PART THREE

THE ADULT STAGE

CHAPTER SEVEN

BUILD YOUR CIRCLE

———

You can only stay a teenager for so long before it's time to grow up and enter adulthood. Transitioning to an "adult" business can feel intimidating, but if you have the right people around you, the shift becomes much smoother.

While some company owners are content with having just one store, I knew I wanted to expand. If you're like me and you dream of opening businesses in other locations, you need to begin identifying the team members who have the potential to take on more responsibility and a bigger role. These people serve a vital role in your growth, as they pick up some of the responsibilities you must leave behind. Select these individuals carefully, because they will form your inner circle, and the strength of your inner circle determines whether your company will grow successfully. If they don't rise to the challenge, your business will suffer.

The management team that makes up my inner circle is comprised of a business partner, two regional managers, and a manager for each individual store. I trust every one of these people on a professional, financial, and personal level. Riverside Pawn deals in valuable assets. We have gold jewelry, diamonds, expensive phones, and other electronics. I tell my team, however, that our company's most valuable asset is our people. As a business owner, you create the company culture. However, the team members in your inner circle stand on the front line most of the time. They need to reflect everything you want your company to be when you're not there.

Although I would love to interact with more of our customers at each store, I simply don't have the time—that has become each manager's responsibility. They create the sort of meaningful relationships that make our customers want to continue doing business with us. I need to trust that each of them will do this with the same degree of commitment and sincerity that I would do it, if I could.

THE IMPORTANCE OF DELEGATION

When a teenager becomes an adult, it can be hard for parents to let go. The same is true of a growing business.

Having an inner circle helped me learn the importance of delegation, but it wasn't easy. Delegating is a difficult skill for many business owners, as they are used to having all of the responsibility.

When I started out, I was the face of my business. Every job, task, and responsibility belonged to me. I paid the bills, cut checks, dealt with customers, and went to meetings. Once you choose to expand, however, you can't do that any longer, because you simply can't be in more than one place at a time. The more locations you have, the less time you'll spend in each store. Someone has to take over the daily decision-making for you.

Delegating means taking a step back and divvying up the tasks among a dedicated and willing team. If you pick the right people, they will want to rise to the challenge of added responsibility. As a result, your workload will decrease, giving you more time to focus on the big-picture tasks.

INVEST IN PEOPLE WHO INVEST IN YOUR BUSINESS

Of course, you don't suddenly wake up one day with a solid inner circle of trustworthy individuals who are ready to help run your business—you have to actively build it. To start that process, look for the quality individuals who already work for you and make sure they stick around.

After all, a quality employee is bound to receive other job offers.

For example, I have a woman in my company who is an especially hard worker, and she's become an incredible team member. A while ago, she approached me and said she'd received a job offer somewhere else. The other job had a higher salary. She said she didn't want to leave Riverside Pawn, but she was under pressure from her family because they needed the extra money. We didn't want her to leave the company either. She was so valuable to us that we offered to match the higher salary offer. I wanted her to be happy and free from any pressure to leave. She stayed with us and is now a trusted member of my inner circle. She is an excellent team member and we are very lucky to have her.

We want our people to invest in Riverside Pawn. Some of our current employees will likely work at the company until they retire. For them, their position doesn't just represent a job, but a career. That's the sort of attitude I want more of my team members to adopt.

Money is obviously a motivator that encourages your inner circle to invest in your business. In our company, we've implemented profit sharing and quarterly bonuses for our top-performing team members. Riverside Pawn doesn't merely split profits between myself and my business partner. It belongs to everyone working there. I reward my team with salaries that are above industry standards and better benefits. If you want the most competent, skilled, and reliable management team, never underestimate the power of financial rewards.

Having said that, money isn't the only factor to consider when building an inner circle. I want my team to grow personally and professionally as well as financially. That takes time. For that reason, I prefer to promote from within, giving greater responsibility to those who earn it. This creates a healthy culture of competition, but it's important that every member of the team feels like they have a fair chance to move higher up the ranks.

DEALING WITH DISAPPOINTMENT

I had an employee who had worked for me a long time, but I didn't feel he was ready to become a manager. At the same time, another employee, who had just begun working for me, quickly proved to be extremely motivated. When an assistant manager position opened up, I chose the second employee for the job. While he had only been working for me for about six months, his drive and determination made him the right person for the position.

I met with the employee who didn't get the job to talk about turning his disappointment into fuel. I wanted him to see the success of his coworker and realize hard work leads to promotion. At first, he didn't take my advice and sulked. Now, however, he has worked his way up to becoming an assistant manager. He bounced back and proved to me he was capable of more. If you promote from within, your team will see that you recognize and reward hard work. They will feel motivated to do better.

CREATE FLEXIBLE SCHEDULES

Another way to build a strong and efficient team is to be flexible with their schedules. Everybody loves flexibility, but some employees need it in order to live healthy lives. For example, I have numerous women in my company who have competing demands because they are also mothers. I love having women in positions of power in my company. In fact, both of my regional managers are women. They are all passionate, honest, and hard-working. However, they also have children and households that they're trying to take care of at the same time.

To accommodate this, I take care to be flexible with their schedules. I understand that their lives don't consist solely of work. If one of their children is sick, I want them to feel comfortable missing work and not worry about getting yelled at. I tell my team to do whatever they need to do, particularly when it means putting their families first. The work will be there when they're ready for it. I never want any of my employees to feel like we're taking them for granted or treating them like machines.

MOTIVATING YOUR TEAM

Building an inner circle of trusted, skilled people is essential. After that, as the leader of that team, you must continually motivate your people. The best way to do that is by involving your inner circle in everything. Your business can't become a one-man show.

TAKE THEIR ADVICE

My team contributes to all of my decision-making, and they're always free to offer their opinions. I don't merely listen in order to appease them. I take their advice to heart. Often, because the management team is on the front line, they know better than me how to implement strategies.

Trust your team and listen to their recommendations. When they feel like they have real input into the direction of the business, they get empowered, and the more you empower your team, the more confident they become. A confident team is a productive team. If my team members come to me with a problem and ask how I would solve it, I turn the question around and ask what they would do. The majority of the time, I tell them to follow their own suggestion.

DON'T MICROMANAGE

Take care not to micromanage. If you leave someone in charge of a specific task, let them do it. Don't get in the way, and never try to act like a puppeteer. You're not pulling the strings, you're letting competent people make their own decisions. Don't try to stop your managers from making mistakes, but treat those mistakes as learning opportunities. In our company, we let each of our store managers set the rules for their store. I don't choose which items they take from customers or how much money they pay or sell them for. Not only do I trust my circle to make these decisions, but they themselves feel confident in making them.

SHOW APPRECIATION

It's vitally important to show your inner circle that you appreciate them and their work. You can do this in a number of ways. First, reward your employees with higher salaries, give them vacation time, and allow them days off. If my team members want to attend an industry event, I make sure to sponsor the trip.

I want every member of my team to feel like they matter. It might be my company, but I want them to share the vision. I have never had to beg an employee to stay. Even when they've received other job offers, my team members want to stay at my company, because they feel valued and respected.

SPLITTING THE RESPONSIBILITY

If you're thinking of expanding your business, it might be time to consider taking on a business partner. That way, you can split the responsibility with someone else. I started working with my business partner, Chad, three years ago. As first, I was hesitant about taking on a partner. Now, I couldn't imagine running the business without him. When I brought him on board, I had three successful stores, and my workload was piling up. I knew Chad because he managed a different pawn shop, but he'd put out the word that he wanted to go into business by himself. A mutual friend introduced us, and we got along well. We had similar ideas about the business and a shared vision, so we agreed to become business partners. Since then, those three stores have grown to seven. I don't think this ever would have happened without our partnership.

With a business partner, you have greater flexibility. I feel more relaxed because Chad and I are on the same wavelength about our company culture. He's just as motivated as I am. We both want Riverside Pawn to thrive and succeed. Because I'm older than him, he views me as a mentor. I've taught him about setting the culture, forming meaningful relationships with team members, and improving customer service. The people he works with absolutely love him, and I couldn't be more grateful to have him. When you find a partner who shares your vision, passion, and goals, your business will thrive.

GROWING WITH YOUR TEAM

If you only have a single brick-and-mortar store, you can run it by yourself. I did it for a while in the beginning. However, once you decide to expand, it's a whole different story. If you dream of creating a big business, you need a strong team of hardworking people to make that happen. As an owner, you're in charge of delegating responsibility to team members you trust.

If you want your inner circle to work as hard as possible, it's your job to motivate them. People work better if they feel their effort is valued, and if they themselves feel cared for. Show your team that you wouldn't be able to run the business without them. Pay them well, offer bonuses, listen to their opinions, and pay attention to their needs. That doesn't mean holding their hands, however. That means making them feel appreciated and giving them enough room to grow and become confident in their decision-making. I guarantee that every single member of your inner circle has something to teach you. Take advantage of that. Learn from them. Your business will benefit, and you yourself will benefit.

CHAPTER EIGHT

READY FOR EXPANSION

Once you have a great team of people in place, and everyone excels at the role they've been assigned, you'll find that the day-to-day running of your business can happen without you. That doesn't mean you should take a back seat and cruise along, however. In fact, you'll most likely be ready to expand even further.

Test your business and your employees. Experiment with how far the company can expand. The more you attempt, the more team members you can employ, the more communities you can reach, and the more people you can help.

ANOTHER TODDLER

When I was sure that my team no longer needed training wheels to successfully run the business, I was ready for our next risk: branching out into multiple stores. Despite feeling ready to expand, we didn't immediately open a second store. The process took time. If you do choose to open in another location, remember that opening a new store means starting from the beginning—the business is reborn.

Whether it's your second time or your tenth, every new store begins as a toddler. It needs parenting, either by you as a business owner, or by one of your main team members. Whoever it is, they need to know your company culture well enough to guide the store through its teenage and adult phases. Many owners fail to realize that when expanding beyond one successful store, they need to go through the same steps that they did the first time. Expanding takes more hard work and sacrifice, but owning multiple stores can be extremely rewarding if you're ready to put in enough time, effort, and energy.

For my company, expanding proved to be an excellent decision, and I haven't looked back. In fact, I've continued to expand. Since establishing our second store, we've made a habit of opening in one or two new locations a year. We don't settle, always pushing our boundaries.

GROWING IN-HOUSE

When we decided to open that second store, we only had four employees. I moved one of those employees to the new store to serve as manager, then I hired two new people to work under him. Now, we had a grand total of six employees working for our company. At that small size, just having store managers was enough to keep things running smoothly.

However, when we expanded again, opening up a third and then a fourth store, it became clear to me that we needed to start hiring specialists in order to maintain our growing company. First, I appointed regional managers, creating a chain of command in which the store managers answered to the regional managers and the regional managers answered to me.

Then, I began to develop our own in-house departments for tasks that we had formerly outsourced, such as payroll and human resources. That gave us full-time employees dedicated to things like paying bills, issuing paychecks, setting protocols, and making training materials and employee handbooks. We also established an in-house internet sales team, which helped us grow exponentially online. We now have three full-time employees dedicated specifically to making sales on websites like eBay and Craigslist.

Bear in mind, as you create new positions and departments within your business, it becomes vitally important that they communicate well, work together efficiently, and that everyone knows their role and where they fit into the company structure.

ONE STEP AT A TIME

Most entrepreneurs have the drive and determination it takes to run a business. Not all entrepreneurs, however, can manage the growth, no matter how motivated they are. Take expansion one step at a time. Growing too quickly can do more harm than good to your business. There have been times when we've bitten off more than we could chew. When we bought out our competitor store, for example, even though it was an opportunity I couldn't refuse, the timing was tricky; we were already in the middle of opening in a new location elsewhere. I remember having a conversation with my dad during that time. As he often does, he asked me how the business was going, so I told him about possibly buying the competitor store.

"That doesn't sound like a smart idea," he said. "Not while you're in the middle of opening a new location. I don't recommend it. I'm not sure you can make it work."

Admittedly, we weren't ready for such a rapid and sudden expansion, but I pressed on. For a while, it stretched us too thin. We didn't have enough team members for both locations, so the ones we did have felt stressed out and overloaded with work. Finally, one of our store managers quit, which meant the rest of the team had to make sacrifices in order to pick up the slack. Eventually, we made it through the rough patch, but it took a lot of hard work and persistence.

Make sure you and your team fully understand what it means to expand. Help them mentally prepare for the challenges ahead of time, so they can manage growth properly. Above all, make sure you have enough people working for you. Without enough people, everyone will feel overwhelmed with the amount of responsibility that expansion entails. Bear in mind, the more you grow and the more stores you open, the more people you need in your inner circle, so make sure you have enough team members for the positions that open up.

As a leader and business owner, your job is to train your inner circle well so they know what's expected of them. If your training is effective enough, they'll be able to pass on those skills to other employees and train new hires. Each member of your inner circle needs to know your company culture inside out. I know for certain that my business partner, regional managers, and store managers value top-notch customer service as much as I do, so they can teach others how the business needs to be run.

SACRIFICING TO GROW

A word of warning: You might have to sacrifice some business in order to grow. I never stopped to consider that a store is more profitable when the business owner is physically present. No matter how dedicated their inner circle is, the owner cares more about the business than anyone else, and their presence makes employees work harder. When I'm managing a store directly, overlooking each transaction, the store performs noticeably better.

When you expand, you give up the chance to be present in your stores on a regular basis. Inevitably, as a result, you might lose some business. Don't panic. Instead, mentally prepare yourself for the fact that your individual stores could suffer when you give up full control. Whatever business you lose on the small scale, however, should be outweighed by the business you gain through expansion.

From the beginning of my business, I made it a priority to know my team members on a personal level. I empathized with their struggles and listened to their needs. When I had five employees, this was easy, as I had the time to talk to and connect with each of them. Now that we have thirty employees, I'm not able to spend one-on-one time with everyone. Again, this responsibility falls into the hands of my inner circle. This, too, has affected business at individual stores. If I could spend more time getting to know every single employee, stores would perform better, but I don't have the time. Still, my managers do a great job of taking over this responsibility, and the overall growth of the company makes up for it.

A HUGE COMMITMENT

Choosing to expand a business is a huge commitment. It's a step that most business owners want to take, but not all have properly prepared for it. Before taking the risk, think carefully about your team members. Do you have enough people to fill all the positions you require? Do you trust your inner circle to take over some of your responsibilities and get them done with the same level of commitment as you?

Don't let the challenge of expansion discourage you. While there are obstacles involved in growing your business, the rewards make it all worthwhile. It's a big leap, but if you wear the right harness, it's a leap you won't regret making.

CHAPTER NINE

EMBRACE YOUR EVOLVING ROLE

When you choose to expand, your business evolves. And, as the business owner, your role in the company evolves too. While you might be used to calling yourself an employee, manager, or leader, expansion leads to so many other responsibilities. Before you know it, you become a mentor, a teacher, a problem solver, and a firefighter—all at once.

When my business had only one location and a handful of employees, I was basically just a manager for the day-to-day operations of a small company. However, when we grew to the point that we had multiple locations with twenty to thirty employees, I realized the need to evolve beyond a day-to-day managerial role to become the CEO of a company.

There are several key differences between a manager and a CEO. As a CEO, rather than managing daily operations, your primary goal is to pave the path of the future of your company. You establish the vision and implement the goals. You set the performance parameters. Not only do you have to lead by example, you also need to enable and inspire your team to lead by example, especially your inner circle.

When you can focus on the big picture as CEO, it helps your team grow and get better. To do that, you have to let go of the day-to-day operations and hand them over to your team. Empower them to take control, so you can pour your energy into the culture and vision.

PUTTING OUT FIRES

In an expanding business, you often find yourself becoming a problem solver. Nowadays, most of my time is spent answering calls from managers. The problems they need help with include everything from power outages to leaky roofs to unhappy customers. The more stores you open, the more problems you have to solve. While you might not want to spend all of your time putting out fires, you have to recognize that even a great management team can't have all the answers. Your team members trust that if they call you, the problem will get solved. If you don't take care of the problem, it's likely that no one else will be able to.

Even though I'm the person my team instinctively calls, I try to involve them in the problem-solving process. That way, if a similar issue arises in the future, they can deal with it without having to consult me. Every now and then, we experience a problem we haven't seen before. In those instances, we brainstorm together. I empower them to help come up with a solution. By doing that, I show my team members that I trust their opinions and feel that they have been trained enough to know how best to approach the situation. Most of the time, their solution fixes the problem. Whatever the issue, stay calm. Look at every challenge as a chance to grow and get better.

My company deals in a lot of firearms, which means we work very closely with the ATF (Bureau of Alcohol, Tobacco, Firearms, and Explosives). When we transfer or sell guns, we're required to fill out the necessary paperwork. Once every three years, we also have an ATF audit. During an audit, ATF agents come into a store and analyze every form we have ever filled out. They check our inventory and make sure we have the number of guns we are supposed to have. One more or one less won't do—we need the exact number.

For a manager, an audit can feel very intimidating, especially if it's unexpected. We've had times where ATF agents turned up for an audit without prior warning. Once, my management team and I were at an airport, ready to fly to an industry convention in Las Vegas, when I received a call from the employee we'd left in charge of our main store.

"The ATF are here," he said.

"What do you mean?" I asked.

"I mean, they're here at the store to do an audit. They just walked through the door."

"Right now?"

"Right now," he said.

The timing couldn't have been worse. The person we'd left in charge of the store had never done an ATF audit before. Clearly, it wasn't an ideal situation, but I embraced it. That audit became a teaching opportunity. Over the phone, I gave my employee step-by-step instructions on what he needed to do and what was required of him. Ultimately, the audit went well, and the ATF agent left satisfied. As an added bonus, my team member was now an expert on ATF audits.

THE EGO TALKING

Some business owners might think that once they've reached a certain level of success, they have nothing left to learn. Wrong—that's the ego talking. Don't become a know-it-all. You don't have all the answers, so don't pretend to. I don't have an immediate solution for every problem that comes our way, but I work through each one with my team. Running a business is trial and error. Keep trying and learn from the mistakes you make.

In business, every step forward means doing something you've never done before. The next store we open will be our eighth. Opening the eighth store is a new experience for us, separate from any of our previous stores. Even though some of the mechanics remain the same, the location, customers, and employees will all be different. We'll experience obstacles we've never seen before. We'll make adjustments we've never had to make before. That's the way it goes with every new store.

No matter how long you've been running your business, or how many businesses you have, you encounter situations you haven't dealt with before. Include your inner circle in every step of the business, and your successes will be that much more rewarding.

FLEXIBILITY IS KEY

Flexibility is key. Although I love being on the front line and talking to customers, that stopped being my primary role once the business expanded. Now, I consider myself a problem solver. I put out fires and handle situations, even those I've never seen before. Instead of lamenting this change, I maintain flexibility and adopt whatever role I need to adopt. Your business is growing, so grow with it. Keep learning with the people around you.

A business rarely stands still. You either improve or get worse, grow or shrink. Since you're going to be moving in some direction anyway, you might as well make the commitment, along with your team, to always move onward and upward. Make your business better today than it was yesterday. Become a better leader today than you were yesterday. Never stop growing, learning, or expanding.

The sky's the limit!

CONCLUSION

Starting my own business wasn't easy. In fact, it remains one of the hardest things I've ever attempted to do. I leapt into the unknown. However, whenever I'm asked if it was worth it, I never hesitate to reply, "Yes, absolutely." I can't imagine where I'd be if I hadn't taken that leap.

If I had decided not to open my business, if I'd given in to the fear and uncertainty, I would have felt an immense amount of regret—a cost I would have had to pay for the rest of my life.

Take the risk. Don't live with the regret.

If you're reading this book, you probably have the mindset of an entrepreneur, in which case, you have a choice to make. Are you going to keep reading books about people taking risks in business, or are you finally going to do it yourself? As soon as you've made the choice to pursue your dream, you've taken the most important step. Everything flows from that initial decision.

IT'S TIME FOR BRICK-AND-MORTAR

Don't get discouraged about opening a brick-and-mortar business in a world dominated by e-commerce. In fact, more than ever, you get to provide the kind of one-on-one human interaction that people crave. Play to this strength. Build relationships with your customers and make them feel appreciated. Have conversations and get to know people.

Remember, you're going into this business to solve problems for your customers, not simply to make money. When you take care of people, the money takes care of itself. Go above and beyond, exceed expectations, and you'll create customers for life.

Yes, opening your own store is hard work, especially during the toddler phase. Make up your mind now, before you even begin, that you're going to stick with it, face the inevitable obstacles and challenges, and work hard every day.

You're going to make mistakes along the way, and occasionally you'll have to deal with problems you never anticipated. You're going to face competition. Sometimes, you'll hire people who don't work out. Social media will occasionally get out of hand. Don't give up, because even your worst experiences can become learning experiences, benefiting you in the long run.

STOP WAITING FOR THE RIGHT TIME

If you dream of owning a business, *you* are the only person who can bring that dream to life. Stop waiting for someone to tell you it's the right time. Don't expect anybody to hold your hand. It's on you now.

That first risk might be the most terrifying, but it's definitely not the only risk you'll ever take in business. At Riverside Pawn, we constantly look for new opportunities. We want to push ourselves in every direction. Our next step is to set up a consulting business for other pawn companies. We're also in the process of creating a website to help entrepreneurs open brick-and-mortar businesses: www.thepawnshopexpert.com.

I had a conversation with my eighteen-year-old daughter recently. She's at a crucial place in her life, out of high school but still trying to figure out what to do with her life. She told me it's ultimately her dream to become a nurse, because she wants to follow in her aunt's footsteps, working in a hospital setting and helping people get healthy.

"That's great," I said. "How do you plan to make that dream happen?"

She hesitated and finally replied, "I don't know. I guess I'll apply to a couple of colleges."

I told her, "It's great to have dreams, but they don't mean shit unless you take action on them. Without action, your dreams can become nightmares, because they'll haunt you."

I shared with her the story of my biggest regret. When I was in school, I dreamed of becoming an astrophysicist and an astronaut, but I never followed through on it. As I mentioned earlier, I wasn't good in school. To this day, I often think about the fact that if I'd just put my head down and taken the necessary steps to realize that dream, my life would be totally different.

I didn't want to feel that same regret in business, which is why I took the leap of faith to start my own company. As I told my daughter, if you have a dream, goal, or vision for your future, put a plan in place to reach it. My daughter isn't going to wake up one day and suddenly be a nurse and have her dream job. In the same way, you're not going to wake up and suddenly own a successful business. Your actions have to make it happen. You have to walk the walk.

Don't let your dream just pass you by. Start taking the necessary steps to make it happen. You already have everything within you that you need to realize your dream. As I told my daughter, it's very much like Newton's First Law: an object at rest tends to stay at rest, and an object in motion tends to stay in motion. It's as simple as taking that initial leap, putting a plan into action, and following through.

If you decide to open a business and work as hard as you can to make it successful, I promise you won't regret it.

ABOUT THE AUTHOR

After dropping out of high school, **JASON WILSON** answered a classified ad for a job at the only pawn shop in town. From those humble beginnings, he climbed the ranks, developed a better way to run the business, and started his own company. Now, he is the owner of Riverside Pawn, a chain of seven stores that does more than $8 million in revenue a year. His passion is to share everything he has learned over the years with new and struggling business owners.

www.ingramcontent.com/pod-product-compliance
Lightning Source LLC
Chambersburg PA
CBHW070932210326
41520CB00021B/6909